Towns and Villages
OF ENGLAND

GOTHERINGTON

THE HISTORY OF A VILLAGE

EDITED BY
DAVID H. ALDRED

GOTHERINGTON AREA
LOCAL HISTORY SOCIETY

ALAN SUTTON

First published in the United Kingdom in 1993 by
Alan Sutton Publishing Limited
Phoenix Mill · Far Thrupp · Stroud · Gloucestershire

First published in the United States of America in 1993 by
Alan Sutton Publishing Inc · 83 Washington Street · Dover · NH 03820

British Library Cataloguing in Publication Data
A catalogue record for this book is available from the British Library

ISBN 0 7509 0591 3

Library of Congress Cataloging in Publication Data applied for

Typeset in 10/11 Bembo.
Typesetting and origination by
Alan Sutton Publishing Limited.
Printed in Great Britain by
The Bath Press, Avon.

Contents

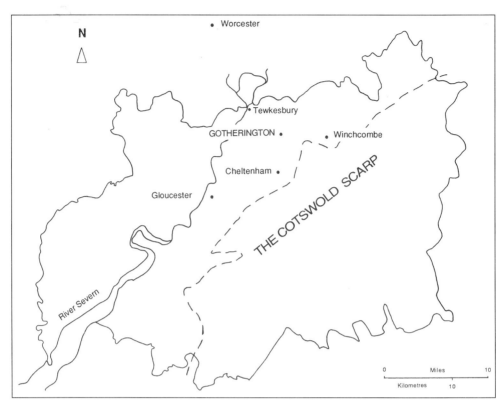

Location map showing Gloucestershire with Gotherington and the main places mentioned in the text

Gotherington in 1965. This view looking east shows some of the earliest phases of the post-war expansion of the village (B. Shelmerdine)

Introduction

'Gotherington is just an ordinary village; it doesn't have any history,' was a comment not uncommonly heard in 1981 when a group of interested people formed the Gotherington Area Local History Society with the aim of investigating the village and surrounding area. This book is our answer to those who felt there was no tale to tell. It comes as the result of an idea developed three years ago when I felt the research carried out by our society's numbers deserved a wider audience than could be reached through the society's *Occasional Papers* and talks at the regular monthly meetings. I hope the following chapters paint a vivid picture of a community based on the land, which has experienced fundamental change since the Second World War. The story is unique to Gotherington but entirely typical of many villages the length and breadth of the country, particularly in this area of north Gloucestershire.

The book is a collection of chapters, written by a variety of local people whose common interest is in the history of the village. We come from many different backgrounds and each chapter reflects our individual styles and interests. My job as editor has entailed cutting down repetitions and narrowing the extreme differences in style to enable the chapters to flow more easily one from another. I have also selected the illustrations. The narrative approach has been adopted as the best way of presenting Gotherington's history to the widest possible audience, consequently the chapters divide the book into recognizable periods, and within each chapter the common themes are discussed. We have always tried to keep alive the wider perspective because we have attempted to write a parish history, not parochial history.

The original intention in writing the book was to bring together all the known aspects of the history of the village. It was not intended to be a book based on pioneering research, and yet, perhaps inevitably, important episodes of the village's history are presented here for the first time: the finds from the Romano-British settlement from the east of the parish; the discovery that Gotherington in the Middle Ages comprised two settlements, not one; and the unexpected find that a late Victorian book of stories is a thinly disguised description of Gotherington life and people at the end of the nineteenth century. Such are often the rewards of ventures into local history.

Gotherington has already been well served by its local historians and we have not attempted to repeat ground already covered by them. Chief among these writers is Owen Stinchcombe whose works on the Board School, Elizabeth Malleson, and the establishment of the Reading Room have added much to the general history of the village. Neither have we attempted to repeat the stories told in Norman Lloyd's history of the Free church, or Marion Holmes' reminiscences of earlier this century which the society published after her death in 1991. We are grateful to them for the ideas they have given us, and particularly to Owen for his early encouragement in our venture.

There are many other people to whom we owe a debt of gratitude. To them all we give our thanks and appreciation, and particularly to the following: Dorothy Brown for gathering much of the information for Chapter 8; Tim Curr for producing many of the photographs; Martin Piercy for annotating the plans. John Postlethwaite played a crucial part in printing off the typescripts, and without Ruth Jones we would have had no typescripts at all. No words of thanks can be too great to Ruth who struggled through the original manuscripts heavily covered with editorial comments. To Eric Reynolds for giving freely of his enormous talent to enrich the chapters with his line drawings we stand similarly indebted. To all of them, and to those who helped in countless other ways, we give our thanks. As editor I would like to thank the contributors for their chapters and their patience as the production of the book took rather longer than originally planned. To none can be apportioned blame for any shortcomings.

To you, our reader, we trust you enjoy the story told in the book and that you will be encouraged to look round the village with a greater awareness of its past. We have given references if you wish to follow up any of the points we have made. Whether you are a long-established resident, a relative newcomer or an interested reader from further afield, we hope we shall be able to convince you that although Gotherington might be an ordinary village, it *does* have a history which is worth knowing. That history unfolds as you turn the next few pages. Please read on.

David Aldred
for the Society
November 1993

NB Measures and money values are quoted in their original form, with no attempt to convert to modern equivalents. For money values 12*d* = 1*s*; 20*s* = £1 = 100p. For area 2¼ acres = 1 hectare.

CHAPTER ONE

Beneath the Soil

A Description of the Geology of the Area and its Links to Human Settlement

Gerald Williams

This history of Gotherington begins with the ground upon which countless generations of inhabitants have lived. It was formed long before human history over a timespan which is almost too great to understand, and yet the area's geology has been important in providing the stage upon which the people have lived, and continue to live, their lives. The rocks and soils add to the visual attractions of the parish. It is a journey of barely three miles from the western edge of the Cotswold limestones on Nottingham Hill, down the steeply sloping scarp above Manor Lane, to the Lias clays of the Severn vale towards Gotherington Fields, and yet within that short distance the land has provided hundreds of acres of arable and pasture, plots for farmsteads and houses, building materials and reliable supplies of water. It has not always looked as it does today, but for the people who have made the area we now call Gotherington their home for over two thousand years, many of their most basic needs for food and shelter have been met by exploiting the ground under their feet.

How was this landscape formed? This is the subject of the first chapter.

THE LANDSCAPE IS SHAPED

Looking westward from the top of Nottingham Hill, across Gotherington, the horizon is interrupted by the Malvern Hills, and to the south-west by May Hill and the Forest of Dean hills. They provide the western edge of the Severn valley and contain some of the oldest rocks in the world, laid down 300 to 500 million years ago, when the earth was still unstable. At that time sporadic buckling and sinking of its crust allowed vast sediments eroded from what are now the uplands of Wales to be deposited in ancient seas and eventually harden into the Triassic rocks which underlie the Jurassic clays and limestones of eastern Gloucestershire.

About 220 million years ago, changes in the climate resulted in the drying up of the lakes and seas, leaving Britain a desert comparable with parts of the Middle East today with the surface being continually swept by violent sandstorms and torrential rainstorms. From the limestone of Nottingham Hill to the blue Lias clays of the vale, the underlying geology of Gotherington was laid in the forty-five million years geologists call the Jurassic period.

Towards the end of this period, about 180 million years ago, subsidence of the land to the south-east was taking place allowing the seas to invade, laying down the limestones, clays and sands of practically the whole of Gloucestershire east of the Severn. The fossilized shells found in the old quarries on Cleeve and Nottingham Hills date from this period, when the limestones of the Cotswolds were being formed under the sea. About 135 million years ago further folding of the earth's surface lifted the Cotswolds out of the sea, forming an escarpment which once lay much further to the west, closer to the Severn or even beyond to the Welsh border country. Over millions of years since the Jurassic period, the escarpment has been eroded away in an uneven manner resulting in the profile seen today and leaving a number of 'outliers' on the plain east of the Severn. Typical examples of outliers in this area are Oxenton Hill together with Crane Hill, Alderton Hill, Bredon Hill, Langley Hill and Dixton Hill.

Within Gotherington, Nottingham Hill is not yet an outlier. Making a conspicuous projection from Cleeve Hill and capped with Inferior Oolite limestone, it is joined to the main plateau by a narrow isthmus crossed by the road from Cheltenham to Winchcombe at a height of 250 metres, and provided a natural defensive site exploited in the Iron Age (see Chapter 2). The gap between Nottingham and Crane Hills has been exploited as a natural routeway (now Gretton Road), and other routeways linked the vale with the Cotswold plateau. Granna Lane still survives as the best example but when these routeways were first developed is not known.

The next period of major change was only some two million years ago. Dramatic changes in the climate took place when temperatures dropped and most of Britain was held in the grip of the Ice Age. The ice-sheets advanced southwards to a line approximately north of the Thames to the Bristol Channel, and although there were inter-glacial periods when the ice receded, the harsh conditions prevailed until about 11,000 years ago. During that time, the area of Gotherington lay on the frozen edge of the ice-sheet which stretched southwards to Bredon Hill and would have looked empty and bare, rather like the open tundra landscapes of Northern Europe and North America today. The eventual retreat of the ice was caused by a gradual increase in the average temperature until about 5,000 years ago, since when the climate has gradually deteriorated. As the ice retreated it left behind vast deposits of boulder clay produced by the grinding of the underlying rocks by boulders carried in the glaciers, and by spreads of gravel deposited in sheet floods as the ice-sheets melted. Much of this is found throughout the Severn valley and today villages from Apperley to Maisemore live on the terraces cut by the Severn as it carried away the melting ice.

Following the retreat of the ice-sheets and an improvement in the climate, the bulk of Britain was covered by deciduous forests providing food and shelter for Palaeolithic (Old Stone Age) peoples who began the long process of woodland clearance.

SANDS AND GRAVELS ARE DEPOSITED

Overlying the lias clays in the Severn vale are to be found areas of 'drift' deposits, i.e. the remnants of the vast quantities of material deposited during the last one and a half million years both during and after the Ice Age. The prime sources of such deposits were glaciation, river flooding and wind erosion. During the Ice Age, the glaciers carried large quantities of boulder clay, sand and gravel, large deposits of which are to be found in the Moreton-in-Marsh area. The lower Severn valley including the Gotherington area was more affected by the melting ice-sheets which caused several floodings of the Severn plain, and deposited huge quantities of boulders, pebbles and gravel over the Lias clay. Rocks and pebbles turned up in local gardens and fields today are the heavier remnants of the flood debris carried down from the Midlands.

Each flood period deposited a new gravel layer in the vale and typical deposits from the second terrace of the original River Avon are to be found extending from Gotherington Fields to the lower end of the village. Deposits are also to be found in Elmstone Hardwicke and Tredington and on the southern side of the road from Bishop's Cleeve to Stoke Orchard where they are at present being quarried.

A third way in which sands and gravel were deposited was by wind. Stretching northwards from Gloucester between the Severn and the Cotswold escarpment are to be found isolated

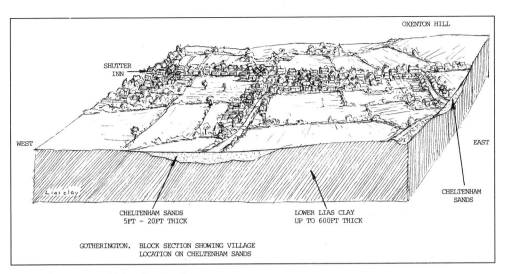

GOTHERINGTON. BLOCK SECTION SHOWING VILLAGE
LOCATION ON CHELTENHAM SANDS

Diagram by Eric Reynolds based on Dreghorn

deposits of sand lying on top of the Lower Lias clay. The make-up of the sand indicated its origins in the sandstones of the Midlands and which was most likely blown here during a dry glacial period between 100,000 and 50,000 years ago. It is quite probable that the sand was widely distributed over the area at this time, and that subsequent erosion and re-sorting by the streams off the escarpment has removed all but the patches of what have become known as the 'Cheltenham Sands'. The sands are to be found in isolated patches of varying thickness, in some places up to 40 feet (12 metres), and lying as they do on the impermeable Lower Lias clay, they provide areas of well-drained land through which the rain-water sinks. In some places they have attracted settlements.

Large deposits are found under Charlton Kings and in parts of Cheltenham stretching north to Prestbury, north-west through Arle and Uckington, and south to Shurdington. Smaller patches exist at Swindon Village, around Kayte Farm between Prestbury and Bishop's Cleeve, at Bishop's Cleeve, Alstone and Alderton. Until recently, the shape of modern Gotherington reflected almost exactly the local extent of the Cheltenham Sands deposits. They are located in the Malleson Road area and much of its growth has taken place through 'infilling' between the older properties and by spreading outwards along the existing belts of sand. Later developments in the eastern part of the village have taken place on the heavier Lias clay, where ground cracking and poorer drainage contrast noticeably with conditions in the lower part of the village. Keen gardeners in the village are only too aware of the difference between the warm light sands and the colder, heavy clays of their garden soils!

WATER SOURCES

The water supplies of today are obtained from the River Severn through the purification plant at the Mythe, Tewkesbury. Before the water-mains were laid, Gotherington depended upon a naturally available reliable supply of water, particularly for watering livestock. Humans can manage with remarkably little quantities for drinking and cooking. In Gotherington, as in other settlements along the western slopes of the Cotswolds, the water supply was of two types, from springs and from wells.

The spring supply came from high on the slopes of Nottingham Hill behind Manor Farm,

Before mains water the settlement was largely supplied by water originating in the marshy ground above Manor Farm where the Lias clay meets the limestone

This modern pump still marks the spot of one of the village wells

issuing from where the limestone of the Inferior Oolite meets the Upper Lias clays. The rain-water seeping through the permeable limestone cannot penetrate the Upper Lias clays, and flows along the junction of these strata to issue from the hillside where the spring is readily identified by the marshy ground supporting a range of wetland vegetation. This spring supplied the farm, and in later years was tapped by a well and pumped over a slight rise in the ground to be gravity fed to a 6,500 gallon (29,500 litre) tank at the farm, from which it was piped to the neighbouring houses in the upper part of the village. It was perfectly adequate under normal conditions although conservation was necessary during the drought of 1921. The other sources of water were the wells which were sunk in the sand deposits beneath the lower part of the village, from which an abundant supply of water was obtained, although its purity gradually deteriorated as the population grew and the increasing accumulation of domestic refuse contaminated the rain-water sinking through the sands.

By contrast neighbouring Woolstone gained all its water from wells, but Oxenton took its water from a spring thrown from the sandy beds on the hillside above Hill Farm, from where it was piped to reservoirs in nearby fields and then to stand-pipes in the village. Dixton Manor was also supplied by a spring issuing from the south side of Dixton Hill, where the water was piped to a nearby tank and gravity fed to the manor.

CONCLUSION

It is difficult to appreciate how slowly geological changes take place, and yet it is the underlying geology that supports the stage upon which human life in the Gotherington area has been enacted. In this chapter time has been measured in hundreds of millions of years; for most of the book it is measured merely in hundreds. It was over 150 million years ago that the limestones and clays of the area were laid down in the ancient seas before being lifted up by the buckling of the earth's surface to form the Cotswold Hills of today.

The limestones of Nottingham Hill have been quarried for building and drystone-walling, the clays of the vale produced the trees for timber in prehistoric times, with pasture for cattle and crops for food as human habitation developed; from this landscape has also come the water necessary to sustain life. A mere 100,000 years ago wind and water brought pockets of sand and beds of gravel to provide the well-drained soils which underlie much of the modern village.

This chapter has covered the geological changes over 500 million years and put into perspective the 10,000 years of known human prehistory and the remaining 2,000 years of human history which form the subjects of the remainder of the book. The uses people have made of opportunities available to them through the natural geological resources have depended upon their needs, technologies and their awareness of these opportunities. The earliest attempts to exploit the landscape form the basis of the next chapter.

References

The following books and publications have been consulted in the preparation of this chapter, and are recommended to the reader who seeks a fuller understanding of the Cheltenham area and the Severn basin.

1   W. Dreghorn, *Geology Explained in the Severn Vale and Cotswolds* (David and Charles, Newton Abbot, 1967).
2   L. Richardson, *A Handbook to the Geology of Cheltenham and Neighbourhood*. Revised by R.D. Beckingsale. (Paul P.B. Minet, Chicheley, Bucks, 1972).

3   L. Richardson, *Wells and Springs of Gloucestershire*. Memoirs of Geological Survey, England (HMSO, 1930).
4   British Geological Survey – Tewkesbury. Sheet 216 – 1:50000 series, 1988. Sheet Memoirs by B.C. Wolsaam, R.A. Ellison and B.S.P. Moorlack, 1989.
5   British Geological Survey – Moreton-in-Marsh. Sheet 217 – 1:50000 series, 1981. Sheet Memoirs by L. Richardson, 1929.

Acknowledgement

I am grateful to Mr Gordon Margretts, Head of the Geology Department at the Cheltenham and Gloucester College of Higher Education in Cheltenham, for initially pointing me in the right direction, and for being kind enough to read and advise on the original manuscript from which much of the material for this chapter has been taken.

CHAPTER TWO

The Earliest Settlers

An Investigation of the Archaeology of the Prehistoric Period

Geoff Newsum

This chapter traces what is known about the Gotherington area between *c.* 10,000 BC and the decline of Roman Britain *c.* AD 450. The evidence we have that people lived in our area is extremely fragmentary and it provides only glimpses of light into the darkness of the unknown. Much use, therefore, has been made of sites and finds outside the present parish, but during this prehistoric period, Gotherington existed neither as a name nor as an identifiable territory, so there are no boundaries to prevent our use of nearby examples.

THE STONE AGES

The thousands of years during which humans fashioned tools and weapons from flints are popularly known as the Stone Age. Flints brought to the area by trade or expeditions from East Anglia and the South Downs survive in the soil and provide the most plentiful evidence for human activity at this time. Unfortunately few worked flints have so far been found in the parish, but this seems more likely to be the result of lack of archaeological enquiry rather than of the lack of prehistoric activity.

The history of a continuous human presence probably starts *c.* 10,000 BC when the Ice Age glaciers finally retreated and the warming climate allowed broad-leaved woodlands to colonize the land, and hunter-gatherer peoples began to exploit the woodlands. From *c.* 6,500 BC people of the middle Stone Age began to clear the woodlands, probably to create corrals to make the hunting of wild animals rather easier.

Finds have been made from around forty scattered locations mainly on the Cotswold uplands. The wide distribution of find spots and the small light nature of the weapon heads, knives, scrapers, awls and blades suggest that the groups were still nomadic hunter-gatherers, travelling around according to the availability of the natural resources and the movement of the herds.[1] Locally finds have been made at Haymes Farm on the lower slopes of Cleeve Hill, and in the vale at Beckford.[2] It would be most unlikely that the Gotherington area also was not being exploited at this time.

During the fourth millennium BC the groups of people living in Gloucestershire began to settle into a less nomadic existence as farming gradually replaced hunting and gathering as the major method of providing food. By *c.* 3,500 BC the final Stone Age period, the Neolithic, was well under way. A main source of information about the life of early Neolithic man in Gloucestershire has been the excavation of several later-built long barrows, revealing that they were built over earlier settlement sites, some of which included rubbish middens and a variety of burial circumstances. Examples are at Crickley Hill, Withington, Hazleton, Notgrove, Swell and, nearest to our own area, at Belas Knap near Winchcombe. Here the later cairn is thought to have been built over two even earlier burial sites, dating from perhaps *c.* 3,500 BC.[3]

The picture painted by this research is one of groups of people clearing small areas of woodland, or extending earlier clearings, to provide land for pasture and growing cereals. Their buildings were supported by posts. They made a simple type of pottery bowl, and flint remained the basis of their tools. The groups were widely dispersed throughout the Cotswolds. The use of long barrows as a resting place for the bones of their ancestors suggests that each group had a clear identity separate from other groups.

The small farming communities prospered and developed. Tim Darvill, one of the country's leading archaeologists and an expert on Gloucestershire, has calculated that by around 2,500 BC there could have been up to two hundred settlements, mostly on the Cotswolds but spreading across the Severn vale to the Forest of Dean. The population may have grown by as much as thirty-fold during the last thousand years.[4] Skills and techniques had also developed. The discovery and excavation in recent years of 'causewayed camps', such as that on Crickley Hill, have revealed what were in essence fortified villages.[5] Advanced building methods had been employed in their construction and the inhabitants had used a greater variety of pottery and finely made flint and stone weapons and implements, some of which had been used with wooden shafts or handles. It is possible that these large camps were bases for arable farming activity on the hills and for the management of valley pastures. The main items of food were cattle, pigs, sheep, wheat and barley.

Perhaps the best known and most numerous legacy from this middle Neolithic period is that of the long barrows. About seventy are known on the Cotswolds, varying in length from thirty to a hundred metres but all of similar location, construction and shape, and most with projecting 'horns' at the wider end creating a forecourt area. Excavations of the barrows and forecourts have revealed many factors to indicate that death was accompanied by beliefs which demanded ceremony and ritual.

Being only about four miles (6 km) in a direct line from Gotherington, Belas Knap is of particular interest. It was, like all long barrows in Britain, built between 3,000 and 2,600 BC, probably over two earlier burial sites as described above. With approximate dimensions of 60 metres in length by 20 metres at the maximum width and over 4 metres in height, the construction says much about the physical and organizational abilities of its builders. Access to the four burial chambers was from the sides of the cairn and the fact that these chambers account for only about one twentieth of the total volume suggests that the barrow had an important visual significance in addition to being a place to bury the dead; perhaps it served as a marker to indicate a particular group's claim to an area of territory, strengthened by the ancestral remains kept safe inside their tombs.

Belas Knap has been excavated twice during modern times, during the 1860s and again in the late 1920s after which its sunken and rather ruinous state was restored to the present condition. The remains of about thirty-eight people were found, the largest number from any long barrow in Gloucestershire but only a fraction of the population who must have been associated with it through many generations. As with all barrows therefore the basic question remains of who exactly qualified for admission.[6]

Medical analysis of remains from the long barrows has revealed that these people were a little over five feet tall and rather long-headed, that they suffered from many present-day illnesses and disabilities and were able to accomplish complex surgical techniques. Common aspects of the long barrow, pottery and tool designs, and the large quantities of flint having to be brought in from its natural sources are indicative of communication networks between groups within the surrounding area and much further afield. Indeed some tools originated in the Lake District, Cornwall and Northern Ireland, an axe found on Bredon Hill came from Brittany, and one from Conderton near Beckford was made of stone which occurs only in Italy or Switzerland.[7]

Belas Knap looked like this before it was rebuilt in the 1930s. The central upright stone is possibly the remains of an earlier burial chamber dating back to *c.* 3,500 BC

Having reached what was at that time something of a peak of development in many areas of skill and social organization, and having enjoyed a period of stability, the Neolithic communities in Gloucestershire were subjected to fairly rapid and possibly catastrophic changes. Some of the camps, such as the one on Crickley Hill, were the scenes of warfare and destruction around 2,500 BC, and many long barrows were blocked up or forsaken. It has been suggested that violence between the communities was caused by food shortages, perhaps after a series of poor harvests, and that the focus of life may have shifted to the valleys.

What, therefore, might the Gotherington area have looked like as the Stone Age drew to a close? Although we are not aware of any credited finds within the immediate confines of the parish, this does not mean that none exist. Perhaps they are there awaiting discovery and certainly pieces of flint can be found quite readily. The hills around the area had quite likely been cleared, and cultivated and clearings, although not necessarily permanent ones, had been made in the vale, quite possibly in our own area. Several known nearby sites have been referred to and appropriate places for clearance and activity would have been linked to any lines of communication which might have existed between them. For example, a route from Belas Knap and sites adjacent to Cleeve Hill, via Nottingham Hill, the end of Gotherington, and the east side of Oxenton Hill to Beckford is an almost straight line. An alternative route following the Tyrl Brook from the foot of Nottingham Hill through our three villages and then to Beckford or Tewkesbury is also a tempting speculation. It is interesting to note that this second route passes the Tibblestone, a pierced standing stone beside the Teddington Hands roundabout just beyond Oxenton.[8] Similar stones in the county are believed to be the remains of long barrows; could the Tibblestone be one of these?

THE BRONZE AGE

Prehistory is divided into 'ages' for the convenience of those who study it, but the divisions between the end of one period and the start of another are very blurred and probably varied

Granna Lane remains in parts a sunken holloway, old enough to be followed by the Saxon boundary, and possibly dating back to Neolithic times

considerably from area to area. This appears to be particularly true in the transition from the late Neolithic to the Bronze Age periods. However, the start of the second millennium BC (2,000 BC) is a convenient marker for the beginning of metalworking, even though the use of flint and stone continued for several centuries. One of the earliest metal objects found in Britain was a small copper axehead from Hawling and early bronze weapons have been discovered on Cleeve Hill.[9] Also from this period, a large number of flint items were found on the lower slopes of Cleeve Hill at Woodmancote, on the same site as the Mesolithic finds mentioned earlier in this chapter, during the excavation of the Romano-British settlement at Haymes.

Round barrows began to replace long barrows as the common form of visual burial and in 1779 Samuel Rudder in his history of the county reported that between Nottingham Hill and Cleeve Hill there were 'four large tumuli or barrows . . . lately opened and found to contain a great quantity of human bones'.[10] Although little remains today to substantiate Rudder's description it provides us with some evidence of human activity on the edge of the present parish.

The excavations of round barrows and other burial sites of the period have revealed many personal ornaments of bone and bronze, finely made and distinctive 'Beaker' pottery (which is sometimes used as a descriptive term for the Neolithic/Bronze Age transition), and new forms of flint and stone artefacts in addition to bronze ones. Some of these appear to have been intended for ceremonial or other non-practical purposes. Overall these finds clearly indicate that 'acquisitive man' had arrived. Several Beaker period sites have been found around our own particular area including pottery at Stanton, burials at Prestbury and on Bredon Hill, and pits containing pottery between Gretton and Toddington only about three miles (5 km) beyond the Gotherington boundary. Some of the long barrows of the earlier age may have remained places of veneration. The ploughed-out site of a round barrow is still visible about a hundred metres from Belas Knap.

Throughout much of the second millenium BC round barrows remained a major form of burial; over three hundred are still visible in the county, mostly on the hills. Aerial photography in recent years has revealed the existence of many more than those with upstanding remains, especially in the Severn valley where centuries of cultivation have obliterated most of the obvious evidence. Grundy's translation of the Saxon charter for Bishop's Cleeve suggests that there were two barrows in the area between Stoke Orchard and Elmstone Hardwicke, although we shall never know what type of barrow they actually were.[11] Another may have covered the burial of a woman in about 1,800 BC found during excavations by the Roses Theatre at Tewkesbury.[12] The barrows and various forms of 'flat' burial were mostly of single occupancy and grave goods tended to be very varied overall but often of the same type, such as weapons in some, tools in others, personal items in others. This could indicate that society had now become more structured, perhaps hierarchical, and with occupational specialisms.[13]

Despite the large number of burial sites and other finds, including evidence of occupational activity at many places, our knowledge of definite settlement locations in the county is very limited through the early and middle periods of the Bronze Age. It is possible that many settlements were fairly transitory and mainly situated in the valleys, perhaps because of a colder and wetter climate and subsequently poor growing conditions on the hills, but that some communities claimed territorial rights on the uplands with the barrows being the visual markers to their claims. Although no evidence for these developments has been found in Gotherington it would be most unlikely that it remained unaffected by them as evidence has been found all around the area.

As the second millennium came to an end (1,000 BC), so did the building of round barrows. The burial of cremated remains in special urns in small cemeteries became the common practice. Some of these cemeteries were marked with standing stones, and Tim Darvill has suggested that some of the ones in Gloucestershire, which were previously thought to have been the remains of long barrows, may have been used for this purpose.[14] Could this have been an alternative (or additional) function for the Tibblestone referred to above? If it was, it would give further evidence that some people were living in or near our area in the vale which was being cleared of its trees.

The distribution of finds and sites suggests that the widespread and perhaps impermanent settlement patterns of the early and middle periods continued into the late Bronze Age. Ditch and bank boundaries may have been constructed as additional markers to delineate ownership of land areas, however, and possible examples have been identified at Beckford and on Cleeve Hill.[15] These features of territorial demarcation, combined with finds of slashing swords and concentrations of arrowheads, suggest strife between the groups.

Could this strife have provided the circumstances giving rise to the discovery of the oldest artefacts so far known from our parish – and the reason for Gotherington's appearance in national surveys? In 1972 two late Bronze Age items were turned up by ploughing on Nottingham Hill within the boundaries of the later Iron Age fort. Subsequent excavation unearthed a hoard of twenty-five bronze objects which had been buried in a wooden box. The most dramatic pieces were three complete broad-bladed swords; there were also four rings with pieces of strap attached, a component for a scabbard, a new form of axehead, a ferrule, a knife, a chisel and an awl. These last two or three items might have been part of a metal craftsman's tool-kit because, in addition, the hoard contained a whetstone, a piece of casting equipment, and several rivets and pieces of wire. This major discovery, on display in the Cheltenham Museum, was equal to all previously known metal finds of the late Bronze Age from the whole of Gloucestershire.[16]

The site, beside Granna Lane, could well have been one of occupational activity as a hearth, a trackway, and several pits (which have not yet been excavated) were also discovered. The finds strengthen the hypothesis that Granna Lane was an important line of communication by this time linking the valley to Cleeve Hill and the routes beyond, for none of the material is available locally. Whether troubled times caused someone carefully to hide

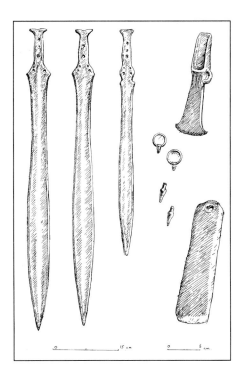

Part of the Bronze Age hoard found on Nottingham Hill in 1972 and now in Cheltenham Museum

their box of treasured possessions and never return for them may be revealed one day by further excavation and research. One simple late Bronze Age arrowhead dug up in the garden of Upper Dix Cottage remains the only artefact discovered within the village to give us evidence of human activity at this time.[17] Maybe other finds have been made over the years but never recorded, and others await discovery.

THE IRON AGE

The troubled times which characterized the close of the Bronze Age appear to have been worsening as the Iron Age dawned in the centuries around 700 BC. It has been suggested that during the previous two or three centuries a deteriorating climate had gradually brought communities down from the uplands and that the acquisition of the cleared and productive foothills became necessary for the survival of an increasing population. Indeed, it may be that the use of iron came about, not as a result of sudden discovery as is often supposed, but because the dislocation of the trading networks hindered easy access to supplies of copper, tin, and lead, and necessitated the use of the more readily available iron ore in western Britain.[18]

This general instability ultimately gave rise to the construction of the hill-forts, perhaps the most notable feature of the early Iron Age, of which about thirty-five are known in Gloucestershire. Two are classified as being large hilltop enclosures rather than fortified camps, and our own Nottingham Hill site is one of these. The discovery of the Bronze Age hoard, described above, suggests that the place may well have been in use before the defences were built. Although excavations have not yet taken place to determine the date of the associated pits, evidence from elsewhere suggests that the site on a natural outlier of the Cotswolds may have been a protected area for keeping food and stock. The Royal Commission on Historical Monuments describes it as:

Nottingham Hill hill-fort with Gotherington in the distance. The hill-fort is cut by Granna Lane. This part of it was created as a result of enclosure in 1806, when the open common was divided into the geometrically shaped fields of today. The surviving ramparts run across the bottom of the picture (Cambridge University Collection: copyright reserved)

> a promontory fort . . . [which] cuts off some 120 acres on a spur of the main escarpment. . . . Two close-set banks, each with an outer ditch, 105 ft overall, cross the spur on the S.E.; the other sides are defined by the scarp edges. The inner bank is placed on rising ground and stands 5 ft above the interior and 10 ft above the inner ditch. The less massive outer bank, springing from the edge of the inner ditch, reaches a height of 7 ft above the outer ditch.[19]

The remaining thirty or so early hill-forts are recognized as having been small settlements, only about one tenth the size of the Nottingham Hill enclosure, strategically placed and with considerable defence systems. Many are situated on the western edge of the Cotswolds and those close to our own area include Crickley Hill, Leckhampton Hill, Buckland, Stanton, Bredon Hill and Cleeve Cloud. It has been suggested that their functions were as clearly visible community bases, from which leaders could oversee their domains and strongholds in times of trouble.

Crickley Hill is the most studied hill-fort in Southern Britain, having been excavated annually since the early 1970s by Professor Philip Dixon of Nottingham. As the evidence suggests that parallels can be drawn between this site and others, a brief account of its history is perhaps appropriate here. The first Iron Age defences were built some time before 650 BC and incorporated the earlier Neolithic settlement. They consisted of a drystone rampart, strengthened with timbers, to a height of over three metres, topped with a wooden palisade and fronted by a ditch more than two metres deep. Two wooden gates shut off the narrow access into the fort which contained six large rectangular houses which were probably built like timber-framed barns with thatched roofs. In addition there were at least twenty-five

The ramparts are now covered with vegetation. This earlier view gives an indication of their scale, although they have been much eroded since the hill-fort was abandoned

smaller structures, many raised off the ground on four posts, probably for the storage of crops, stock and implements. The community did not last long; within less than a century the walls had been breached and the gates and buildings burned.

After some years of abandonment, the walls were rebuilt and increased and new gates were inserted, protected by huge stone bastions and an outer gate. Inside the fort a massive roundhouse was constructed, over fifteen metres in diameter, surrounded by smaller roundhouses and a variety of other structures similar in shape and purpose to those of the earlier fort. The differences in building techniques and pottery finds suggest that the second group of settlers were newcomers, perhaps from the other side of the Cotswolds, but their occupation was equally short. Probably soon after 500 BC the fort was attacked and taken, and the buildings burned, but this time it was not rebuilt.[20]

Other hill-forts may well have had similar histories, although not always with the same chronology. For example, the Leckhampton Hill rampart is known to have been burned, the Bredon Hill fort was the scene of battle and destruction, and it was necessary to double the original rampart on Cleeve Cloud.

Although clearly conjecture, it is possible to speculate on the territory ruled from the Cleeve Cloud hill-fort. Earlier this century excavations at the King's Beeches and Stables' Quarry areas on the hill revealed finds of pottery, postholes and fragments of daub from dwellings. There were also the remains of cattle, sheep and pigs, all indicating settlement close to the fort.[21] The Nottingham Hill enclosure described above, being only a short distance away, is more likely to have been associated with it rather than in opposition to it, possibly used for holding animals rather than an area of extensive settlement.

Could such a territory have extended to Oxenton? For many years the area known as 'The Knolls' was regarded as another hill-fort and an excavation in 1931 produced a quantity of Iron Age pottery. However, the RCHM survey of 1976 discredited the hill-fort theory, showing the site to have natural scarp drops on all sides except one where there is certainly a low bank but no definite signs of fortification. If, then, the Knolls was an undefended or minimally defended settlement, did it look to Cleeve Cloud for its centre of power and

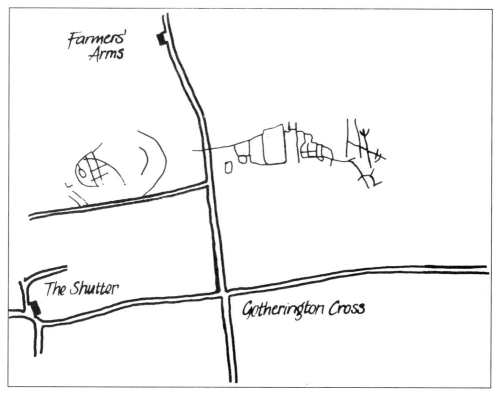

A sketch plan of the soil marks to the west of the modern village. Surface finds indicate they go back to the Iron Age. They seem to show small enclosures and linear boundaries

protection? The pottery finds might provide another indication of links between these sites. At Cleeve Cloud, King's Beeches, Stables' Quarry and the Knolls, the early Iron Age had scant representation. Most of the sherds were of similar design and dated from the middle period (400–100 BC).[22] Clearly they were all in use at the same time and making or acquiring the same types of pottery. This also shows that the sites were still being used after about 400 BC when many other hill-forts had been abandoned in favour of a few much larger but less fortified constructions such as Uley Bury and Salmonsbury Camp, Bourton-on-the-Water. There is evidence that the Bredon Hill fort was refurbished and occupied during this middle period and the excavations at Beckford showed that, by this time, the settlement in the vale had developed in size and activity to that of a small village, but significantly not on the same site as the present village.[23]

The closeness of our area to the Beckford settlement, and the suggested importance of Granna Lane and its extended line as an important route between local sites and then to other parts of the country, have already been referred to. It could therefore be significant that, among the pottery found at The Knolls, were pieces of containers used to transport salt from the Droitwich district. Such discoveries serve to remind us that at all times in their history, the people living in our area did not live their lives in isolation from other communities.

There is one more known Iron Age site in Gotherington. The RCHM survey refers to rectangular enclosures with partly-overlapping ditches, covering approximately one acre, about one mile south west of the village.[24] Aerial photographs show several acres of soil marks and ditches in the fields on the south side of the track leading from the Evesham Road to Longfurlong caravan park and continuing on the other side of the road. Several sherds of pottery from the middle Iron Age have been found on the surface. If future investigation shows this site to be contemporary with those on Nottingham Hill and The Knolls, we have another example of a settlement in the vale most likely linked to one or more settlements on the hills, probably set into identifiable territories.

As the middle Iron Age progressed and the hill-forts decreased in importance, settlements developed in the valleys. The Gotherington site referred to above could prove to be such an example, and another was discovered in Bishop's Cleeve in 1989. Finds made during the initial stage of the housing development on Gilder's Corner led to emergency excavation work which revealed pottery dating from *c.* 300 BC (including pieces of salt containers similar to those found at The Knolls), a contemporary finger ring and brooch, and a variety of settlement ditches plus pits which were probably for storing grain.[25] As Iron Age pottery is known to have been found in the School Road/churchyard area of Bishop's Cleeve early this century, it is possible that much of the central core of the village could overlie a large settlement located on a raised patch of Cheltenham Sand, similar to the one at Beckford.

The finds from the early and middle periods of the Iron Age reveal much about the lifestyles of the communities who lived around our area. The wide range of animal bones, burnt grain, querns for milling flour by hand, and storage sites, show that the inhabitants lived by mixed farming. A high incidence of sheep bones combined with loom weights and weaving combs point to the importance of textile production, and many localities produced their own pottery. Other pottery, stones for querns and whetstones, and glass beads for personal adornment, all indicate trade from further afield, possibly via the River Severn.[26]

During the last century BC contact between the south of England and Europe appears to have increased dramatically as the advance of the Roman empire brought about new needs for trade and perhaps support. By the early years of the first century AD the south east of England up to the Thames valley had become particularly affected by this contact and had begun to take on some of the urbanizing influences from the Continent. The present county of Gloucestershire, being on the edge of this zone, was probably subjected to a 'knock on' effect and drawn into the influence of the expanding Roman empire. However, other than the introduction of coinage by the ruling Dobunni tribe, there is little evidence of change in the late Iron Age communities living in and around the Gotherington area.

THE ROMANO-BRITISH PERIOD

After Julius Caesar's famous sorties to Britain in 55 and 54 BC, invasion was abandoned for about a hundred years. Trade with the Continent continued and when the Roman army of occupation arrived in AD 43 the cooperation of the agricultural communities was encouraged, although resistance was dealt with where necessary. The Dobunni may have been one of the tribes which formally surrendered to the Emperor Claudius and, within three or four years, most of the south-eastern part of England from the Humber to the Severn had been occupied. The Fosse Way was built to run along this frontier.[27]

Three places in Gloucestershire became early military sites. At Cirencester a fort was built some time between AD 50 to 60 and occupied for about twenty-five years by a cavalry unit of five hundred men, probably to control the area previously ruled by the Dobunni from Bagendon a few miles to the north. At a similar date a fort was established at Kingsholm on the outskirts of the modern city of Gloucester, to be replaced about fifteen years later by a new fort in the present city centre. This was occupied until the late '70s.

Once an area had been conquered, the existing population was Romanized and brought under the rule of Rome. It was the Roman practice to establish strategically placed towns under the control of civilian officials in order to maintain domestic and economic stability and to influence the local population peacefully into Roman ways. The early military forts and their surrounding settlements were often used as the bases for these towns, and this was the case in Gloucestershire.

Gloucester (Glevum) appears to have been founded during the last decade of the first century. The rampart of the original fortress was strengthened as the early town developed within the familiar playing-card shaped defences with gates near the centre of each side. Gloucester eventually contained all the typical features of a Roman town with a range of official buildings, colonnaded streets, a forum, basilica, temples, baths, grand centrally-heated houses with mosaic floors and courtyards with fountains, and the shops, humbler dwellings and trade and work premises to service the needs of the inhabitants. Many of the latter spilled beyond the walls and into the surrounding area as the population grew.

Although the original military site was used at Cirencester (Corinium), it appears that a completely fresh start was made on the town with the first of the grid-system streets being laid out between AD 75 and 100. The defences were not built until a hundred years later. There were similar civic and private buildings and facilities to those at Gloucester and, as Cirencester became the provincial capital, it probably contained the governor's palace. One home belonged to a family of such wealth and importance that it contained the finest set of mosaics to be found in a single house in Britain and, outside the town, an amphitheatre provided additional entertainment for up to six thousand people.

Throughout the second, third and fourth centuries both towns were subjected to considerable changes as buildings were altered, extended, adapted, or demolished and rebuilt in accordance with the fashions and needs of the times.[28] In this respect Roman town life had much in common with town life today, and the extent of the changes that took place is not surprising in view of the fact that the Roman occupation was a similar period of time to that which has elapsed since the reign of Elizabeth I to the present.

In addition to the important towns of Gloucester and Cirencester a number of major settlements developed which, although often of considerable size and having some of the sophisticated features of urban living, remained essentially agricultural in character. Some of these may have started as early military forts, others may have been established as administratively convenient locations especially for the collection of corn tax. The most important of these rural settlements to be discovered so far were at Dorn near Moreton-in-Marsh, Bourton-on-the-Water, Lower Slaughter, Dymock, Kingscote, and Wycomb (Andoversford). The closest to Gotherington was probably the one in the Oldbury area of Tewkesbury.[29]

Another form of rural settlement was the villa. About fifty are known in the county but many more probably await discovery. They were usually the homes of owners of large agricultural estates and built to high specifications of Roman style and comfort with central heating, bath suites, mosaic floors, and decorated plaster walls. Most of the villas were built during the third or fourth centuries, although the one at Chedworth was started earlier. Woodchester villa was virtually a palace, and the Gloucestershire area was clearly an important one politically and economically attracting the people of wealth and status who lived in the villas.

Close to our own area, two villas were excavated during the last century in the hills behind Winchcombe. Spoonley Wood villa was built on three sides of a central courtyard. It contained heated rooms, a bath suite, mosaic floors mostly of geometric designs, and a veranda fronting the main side containing the living quarters. Finds included many third- and fourth-century coins, window and decorative glass, a variety of pottery and iron implements, and a bronze bowl. Wadfield villa was of similar plan to Spoonley but more compact and probably

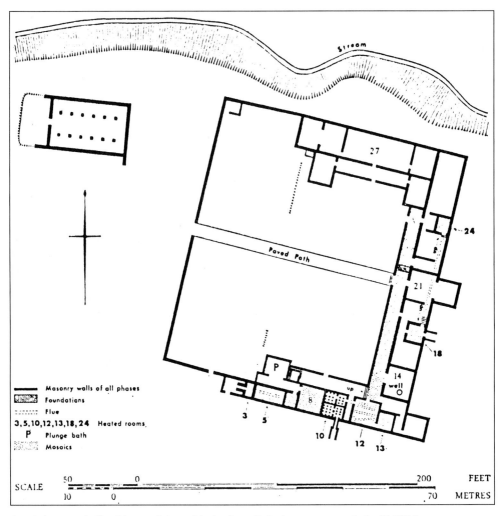

A typical courtyard villa of the area. It is possible the site at Gotherington was very similar (RCHM)

not built in a single phase. Remains of the usual mosaic floors, bath houses, and painted plaster walls were discovered but small finds were limited to a few coins, coarse pottery and some items of jewellery. In 1969 another building, a skeleton and Roman pottery was found about fifty yards from the villa. Coins and pottery have also been found at the Belas Knap long barrow nearby suggesting that the site was a place of interest, perhaps even one of veneration, during the Roman period. Various other stray finds have been made in the areas round the two villas, and at Coles Hill, a little further down the valley from Spoonley, the discovery of a carved eagle, an uninscribed altar stone, a quantity of coins and jewellery, and several burials have indicated that the site could well have been a shrine.[30]

It has been suggested that, during the third century, a decline in trade with the Mediterranean and a change in the taxation system forced the province of Britain to be more self-reliant. This promoted domestic trade and production under which the rural settlements flourished. The greater focus of attention and resulting higher status of the rural areas caused them to become more Romanized, blurring the divisions between town and country. During the fourth century the villas in the country developed the standards of luxury formerly lavished on the fine town houses as the mosaicists, potters, and other artists and craftsmen moved to these new areas of opportunity. An additional suggestion is that many of the Roman villa-estates and villages that we know about are ones which were economic failures. The very fact that they have been available for discovery, in open country, points to their failure; the successful ones continued as centres of population and lie under some of our present-day villages.[31]

Despite the Romanization of many larger rural settlements and villa-estates there were numerous smaller settlements and individual farmsteads which were probably little affected by the occupation, especially during the first century or two. People continued to farm the land in much the same way as they had done during the Iron Age, often at the same sites, but making a certain amount of use of the coinage and new 'consumer goods'. Much of the early Roman pottery is archaeologically indistinguishable from that of the late Iron Age.

This may well have been the situation around our own area. The RCHM survey refers to earlier reports of Dubonnic and Roman coins, a lance head, and stone coffins and skeletons being found (and since lost) at the Nottingham Hill camp. A little pottery and three coins came from the Stables' Quarry and King's Beeches sites on Cleeve Hill respectively, and the Gilder's Corner excavation revealed first and second-century ditchwork, a needle and pin, and two burials from the same period.

Further evidence of occupation in Bishop's Cleeve was discovered during the construction of the bypass, and during the late 1970s and early 1980s Bernard and Barbara Rawes excavated the Haymes Farm site at Woodmancote prior to the construction of the reservoir. As was described earlier in the chapter flint finds showed occupation during the Stone Age, and Iron Age pottery suggested that the place had been in use in periods before the Romans arrived. Coins from the early second to late fourth centuries indicated almost three hundred years of Romano-British settlements, and the excavations painted a picture of a farmstead whose early timber and thatch buildings were replaced by wooden-framed ones on low walls and with tiled roofs. The farm probably had a mixed economy; cattle, dog and sheep bones were present in some quantity and pig and deer bones showed that use was made of neighbouring woodlands.[32]

As in the earlier periods of prehistory, evidence of human activity in the Gotherington area is very slight and our assumptions are based on parallels from nearby locations. A few sherds of Romano-British pottery have been picked up in the same area as the Iron Age pottery near the caravan park. However, in 1984, the best evidence for a site occupied during the Roman period was discovered in the south-east corner of the field opposite the end of Granna Lane, bordered on the south side by the road to Gretton and on the east side by an arm of the Tyrl Brook. Although no excavations have taken place the area was fieldwalked several times revealing a concentration of building-sized stones around the centre of the site, some of which were reddened by fire. In this central part were found two pieces of quern for grinding corn. Scattered relatively evenly over the whole area were a few items of unidentified and undated bone and metal, pieces of tile, a fragment of painted plaster, and a vast quantity of pottery sherds. The finds indicated a Romano-British farmstead of some size and quality.

Samples of the pottery were identified and dated by Bernard Rawes, and by Dr Jane Timby of the Gloucester Excavation Unit. The bulk of it was from the second and third centuries, some possibly as early as the Iron Age/Roman transition period, and some perhaps from the final Roman phase in the fourth century. The site was clearly occupied for a long time.

Most of the pieces were from an infinite variety of shapes and sizes of ordinary pottery for a multitude of general purposes in the life of the farmstead. However, some were from small, fine, decorated items for eating and drinking or holding small measures; other large, thick

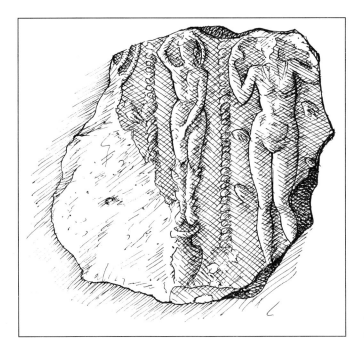

The sherd of Samian ware
described in the text

sherds belonged to massive storage vessels. Fragments pierced with many small holes were parts of colanders and pieces with coarse grit embedded in the inside surfaces were the remains of grinding mortars for culinary or perhaps medical use.

Although the greatest proportion of the pottery used on the farmstead was the local Severn valley ware, other places of origin with their own distinctive types included the East Midlands, the Malvern area, Cambridgeshire, Oxfordshire and Dorset. Several sherds of continental pottery, the famous and high-quality red Samian ware, were also found of which the most exciting discovery was a decorated piece about five centimetres square. This was examined by Bernard Rawes who produced the following detailed report:

> This is part of a bowl called a form 30 made in Lezoux in Central Gaul from about 160 to 190 AD. The central zone shows two nude female figures which probably represent the goddess Venus. They were used by a group of potters whose kilns were at Lezoux in what can be called the workshop of Cinnamus. It is quite likely that this piece was made by a potter called Divixtus. The figures stand between bead rows with small leaves in the background. Part of a double-lined swag appears in one corner. Decorated Samian often has the potter's name stamped on the base. Thus we are able to date it with some precision.[33]

To learn such details, including the likely name of the potter, was a considerable bonus for those of us who took part in the fieldwalk and experienced the thrill of finding things that had belonged to previous inhabitants of the area about sixteen hundred years ago. At such times we wondered about those people. As they stood in their fields and looked around, we imagined a landscape of fields, open ground and woodland much the same as today. We wondered when they abandoned the site and under what circumstances? Was it fear during the less settled times at the end of the fourth century, or was it for unknown social, economic, or even family reasons? We shall possibly never know the answers to these questions. What is clear, though, is that the later settlement of Gotherington did not grow up here on the edge of the territory, but away to the west, more towards the centre, for which we have no evidence of a settlement in this early period. How and why such changes took place are explained in the next chapter.

References

1 T. Darvill, *Prehistoric Gloucestershire* (Alan Sutton Publishing and Gloucestershire County Library, Gloucester, 1987), pp. 28–32.
2 A. Saville (ed.), *Archaeology in Gloucestershire* (Cheltenham Art Gallery and Museums and the Bristol and Gloucestershire Archaeological Society, Cheltenham, 1984), pp. 75–6.
3 T. Darvill, op. cit., gives more detailed information – see pp. 24–40 and 49–62.
4 Ibid., p. 40.
5 P.W. Dixon and P. Bourne, *Crickley Hill and Gloucestershire Prehistory* (Crickley Hill Trust, 1977), pp. 1–5.
6 The latest thinking is based on the excavation of the Hazleton long barrow by Alan Saville between 1979 and 1982. He estimated it might only have been used for a century from *c.* 2,950 BC. Thirty-two adults and nineteen children were buried there. He suggested the long barrow might have contained all the remains of one family over a short period of time. Once their claim to the land had been accepted, the barrow was abandoned. The Corinium Museum in Cirencester has a display of the excavation.
7 T. Darvill, op. cit., p. 63.
8 In recent years the Tibblestone has been removed from its former position which was on the opposite side of the road at the crossroads, now replaced by the new roundabout. See Chapter 3 for more details.
9 A. Ellison, 'Bronze Age Gloucestershire: Artefacts and Distributions', in A. Saville (ed.), op. cit., pp. 115–17.
10 S. Rudder, *A New History of Gloucestershire* (original publication 1779; reprint by Alan Sutton Publishing, Gloucester, 1977), p. 369.
11 G.B. Grundy, *Saxon Charters and Field Names of Gloucestershire*, Part 1 (Bristol and Gloucestershire Archaeological Society, Bristol, 1935), pp. 74, 75.
12 A. Hannan, *Beneath Tewkesbury's Buildings* (Tewkesbury Borough Council, n.d.), pp. 6–7.
13 For wider and more detailed information see: T. Darvill, op. cit., pp. 95–108 and J. Drinkwater and A. Saville, 'The Bronze Age Round Barrows of Gloucestershire: A Brief Review', in A. Saville (ed.), op. cit., pp. 128–39.
14 T. Darvill, op. cit., p. 110.
15 D.H. Aldred, *Cleeve Hill: The History of the Common and its People* (Alan Sutton Publishing, Stroud, 1990), pp. 8–9.
16 A. Saville (ed.), op. cit., pp. 123–4; T. Darvill, op. cit., pp. 118–19.
17 Personal communication with Dr G. Pitt.
18 T. Darvill, op. cit., p. 124–5.
19 RCHM, *Iron Age and Romano-British Monuments in the Gloucestershire Cotswolds* (London, 1976), p. 59.
20 P.W. Dixon and P. Bourne, op. cit., pp. 6–13.
21 D.H. Aldred, op. cit., pp. 10–13.
22 A. Saville, op. cit., pp. 152–6.
23 J. Wills, 'Excavations at Beckford', lecture at Parmoor House, Cheltenham, 5 November 1990.

24 RCHM, op. cit., p. 59.
25 C. Parry, 'Gilder's Corner, Bishop's Cleeve: Post-Excavation Report', lecture at Gotherington Village Hall, 15 November 1990.
26 T. Darvill, op. cit., pp. 45–51.
27 A. McWhirr, *Roman Gloucestershire* (Alan Sutton Publishing, Gloucester, 1981), pp. 59–80.
28 For fuller details of the founding and development of Cirencester and Gloucester, see A. McWhirr, op. cit., pp. 5–58.
29 Ibid., pp. 59–80.
30 RCHM, op. cit., pp. 112–15.
31 R. Reece, 'The Cotswolds: an Essay on Some Aspects and Problems of Rural Settlement', in A. Saville, op. cit., pp. 182–9.
32 D.H. Aldred, op. cit., pp. 15–17.
33 Personal communication from Bernard Rawes, 12 March 1985.

CHAPTER THREE

'*Guthere's* Farmstead'

Gotherington in Anglo-Saxon Times

Phyllis Jones and Jill Collins

This chapter takes us from the decline of Roman Britain to the arrival of the Normans in England. In these years the area received its present name. Our earliest documents also date from this period. From them we can begin to put together a history of the people.

By the time the Roman armies withdrew from Britain in the early fifth century, the province of Britain was suffering a severe economic decline. By the mid 400s the Romano-British villas and towns were falling into decay. Archaeological investigation has shown that the last remnants of the population of the provincial capital Cirencester had abandoned the town and were living in timber buildings in the amphitheatre. Gloucester also was in decline with its buildings in disrepair.[1] It might have been at this time that the Romano-British farmstead near Granna Lane fell out of use, caused by the depressed times coupled with a fall in population which did not recover in size until the tenth century.

The Anglo-Saxons first conquered and settled south and eastern England, then gradually over a period of two centuries progressively subjugated the rest of the country pushing westward as far as the Severn. The defeat of three British kings at Dyrham near Bath in 577 by Cuthwine and Ceawlin gave them the remnants of Gloucester, Cirencester and Bath and opened up the Severn valley to Saxon control.[2] It is now thought the numbers of invaders were small and that they took over the existing population as rulers.

THE EMERGENCE OF GOTHERINGTON

We have not yet found any evidence in or around modern Gotherington for what happened locally in these years, but in 1968 twenty-seven skeletons were excavated from a cemetery of the mid-sixth century near Lower Farm in Bishop's Cleeve, near the modern bypass. The bodies were clearly those of pagans, having been buried with grave goods. The cemetery signifies that the Saxons had reached our area possibly even before the battle of Dyrham, but it was on the very edge of the known area of Saxon control by this date, and the only cemetery yet found off the Cotswolds in the Severn vale.[3] Perhaps the community was living peacefully among the existing British population. Unfortunately we only know where they were buried, not where they lived.

The present area of Gloucestershire was rapidly incorporated into the English midland kingdom of Mercia in 628 under its pagan king Penda. It is believed that it was he who combined the Angles and Saxons of the Severn valley into a single lordship and that he created the under kingdom of the Hwicce which is known to have existed within a generation of his death.[4] The kingdom of the Hwicce, which existed from about 630 and

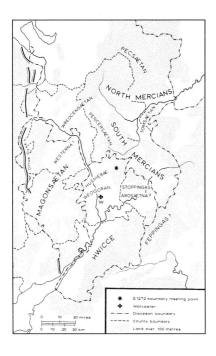

The map from Della Hooke's book *The Anglo-Saxon Landscape* showing the position of the territory of the Hwicce (By kind permission of the author)

included Gloucestershire (without the Forest of Dean), the whole of Worcestershire and south-east Warwickshire, was a small subject kingdom of Mercia. Their princes were believed to be Angles from the Avon valley. They were viceroys or sub-kings, semi-independent rulers who granted land with the consent of the Mercian kings. In the early years they were great princes but as time passed by about 800 they had slipped in status to the level of 'ealdorman', the equivalent of an earl. The Hwiccan princes were Christian by 600 and the kingdom was a bishopric by 679. Offa, who ruled from 757 to 796, was the greatest of the Mercian kings. He corresponded on equal terms with Charlemagne. His coinage based on the Frankish system of twelve pence to the shilling and twenty pence to the pound has only just been superseded. In Gloucestershire he created a great earthwork or dyke to form a defensive boundary against the Welsh. Even today its remains are impressive. During this same period, Christianity was being reintroduced into Britain and within one hundred years the whole country was organized into bishoprics with churches. The diocese of Worcester (which included the present diocese of Gloucester) was formed in 679 to serve the kingdom of the Hwicce. Throughout the diocese, the Hwiccan rulers set up minster churches on their estates. From these churches small communities of priests worked to christianize and then minister to the surrounding population. By 800 there were more than a dozen in Gloucestershire including Beckford, Winchcombe, Cheltenham, Deerhurst and Tewkesbury as well as Bishop's Cleeve. Although King Offa and Aldred stated in the preamble to the Bishop's Cleeve charter that they were giving land to the church to gain relief for their souls and riches in heaven, there were often other more prosaic reasons for founding a minster. One was that the land granted to a minster enjoyed certain tax advantages, while remaining very much the personal possession of the family who expected to be able to bequeath it to their relatives, women as well as men. This provided a powerful influence in the community supporting the interest of the founder. Whatever the reasons, so much land was given to the church that by the end of the eighth century about a quarter of all the land in Gloucestershire had passed into ecclesiastical hands. In their turn the lesser lords built chapels for their subjects, and in time chapels appeared in

Bishop's Cleeve parish church is mostly medieval, but it stands on the site of the Saxon minster

Upper Gotherington, Southam and Stoke Orchard, as these manors were subdivided from the great estate of Bishop's Cleeve.

The history of Gotherington in the Anglo-Saxon period is inextricably bound up with that of Bishop's Cleeve. The land on which Gotherington stands seems likely to have been part of a royal estate granted by a Hwiccan ruler to support a minster church in Bishop's Cleeve before 777–9.[5] We can assume this because in those years a further grant of land was made to the church by Aldred, sub-king of the Hwicce, and Offa, King of Mercia. This was of an area of land associated with a settlement called *Timbingctun* which seems to have been near or under modern Southam. Both grants were made out of a larger estate which belonged to the king, and both were described as fifteen hides in extent. (A hide was traditionally the unit of land which could support a family, but by this time it was usually used as a unit of taxation.) The minster was dedicated to St Michael the Archangel and was built *aet clife*, a reference to the cliff which also gave its name to Cleeve Hill. The extent of the estate of Bishop's Cleeve entered in the Domesday Book is thirty hides. Dr Steven Bassett of Birmingham University has shown how it was substantially the same as the combining of the two earlier estates; certainly the area of Gotherington was included within its boundaries. By 899 the minster had failed and the land came into the hands of the Bishops of Worcester and remained there until the sixteenth century. This became the ancient ecclesiastical parish of Bishop's Cleeve which also included Brockhampton, Southam, part of Stoke Orchard and Woodmancote. Two eleventh-century copies of the Saxon charter exist. From their boundary description it is possible to trace the boundary of the estate today using the landmarks and natural features described in the charter. The northern boundary is still the present day boundary between Gotherington and Woolstone which in part follows the Tyrl Brook.[6]

The description of this northern boundary can be followed from a spot called the Black Pond (*Blacan Mere*) which is where the west boundary of Gotherington meets the Dean Brook about half a mile south-south-west of Gotherington Fields Farm. It then follows the line of the Old Dyke or *Ealden Dic* to a small stream. The old dyke or ditch was evidently manmade

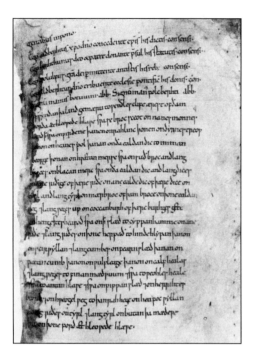

Part of the eleventh-century manuscript describing
the boundaries of the estate attached to Cleeve. The
description of the boundary around Gotherington
comes in the centre of the page (By permission of
the British Library: Cottonian Tiberius A XIII 24)

The hedge cutting across the middle of the photograph marks the western extremity of Gotherington's territory at
Gotherington Fields. Its straightness signifies its artificial nature – 'the old dyke'

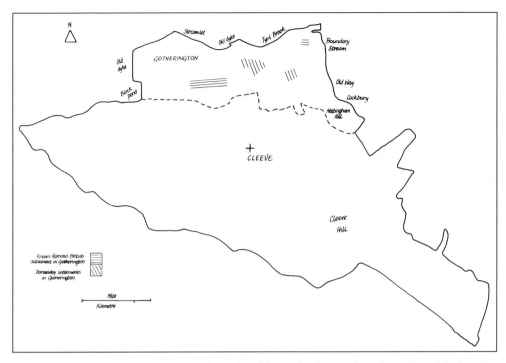

The Saxon boundary followed the present northern edge of the parish. The map shows the position of the boundary markers

to mark the west boundary and seemed 'old' by the eleventh century. The streamlet described as the *Rithig* is the brook which forms the west part of the north boundary of Gotherington. It can easily be seen today crossing under the A435 halfway between Gotherington Cross and Woolstone Turn. The boundary continues along the stream to the two modern semi-detached houses in Woolstone Lane, then down the hedgeline diagonally in front of the houses to join the Tyrl Brook. It then runs along the Tyrl except where the stream makes a short detour round the field called Upper Millham where it was diverted in the medieval period to form a mill-race for a now vanished watermill on the Woolstone side of the stream. The site of the mill is marked by two odd mounds in the corner of a field. Close to Dixton the Tyrl is joined by a small stream which runs down a valley next to Granna Lane. This valley is called the Merecombe, which means boundary valley, and the stream is described in the charter as the *Maerbroc* or boundary stream. A house in Granna Lane called The Merecombes perpetuates the name. The boundary follows this stream to its source, then continues south to the Old Way – Greenway (i.e. Granna Lane) in the later eleventh-century copy – as it rises to the plateau on Nottingham Hill, which is referred to as *Coccan Burh* the old name for the hill which survives today in the names of Cockbury Court and Rushy Cockbury.

The existence and survival of these two land charters mark a significant stage in the history of Gotherington. For the first time we have clear evidence that the landscape has been divided into territories. The area of Gotherington was included in the larger territory attached to the church at Bishop's Cleeve, thus providing a thread of continuity right through to the twentieth century. The boundaries of this territory around Gotherington were probably newly made in the Anglo-Saxon period, for they pass so close to the Romano-British farmstead near Granna Lane that it is tempting to believe its ruined buildings were used as a

29

boundary marker, but in so doing the boundary must have separated the farmstead from some of its fields, and must have been a new boundary.

These two documents make no reference to Gotherington itself, but this need not surprise us because it was the territorial boundaries which were important, not the people who lived within them. The two settlements which are mentioned, *Timbingctun* and Cleeve itself are included only so that people knew where the estates lay, and it was not necessary for other places to be named.

Two pieces of evidence do, however, suggest Gotherington was in existence by 777–9. Its name means 'farmstead associated with Guthere'. *Timbingctun* means 'farmstead associated with Tymba'. From the similarity of their names it is not unreasonable to suppose it belongs to the same historical period, i.e. before the late eighth century when we know *Timbingctun* was in existence. The second piece of evidence comes from the charter grant itself. The Hwiccan kings granted to the minster church of St Michael, not the land, but the profits from the land. The land at Gotherington is on the edge of the territory, yet it was included. Wealth could be gained from it, and people were needed to create wealth.

Further evidence that people were living at Gotherington can be drawn from the processes by which it came to be divided manorially from Bishop's Cleeve. The first stage was the separating of the whole territory of Gotherington in return for the lord to provide a horseman, or knight, for the king. This obligation provides a useful clue to the development of the community, for when the territory was further subdivided into Lower and Upper Gotherington this obligation was split into half. As Lower Gotherington was split further, so too was the obligation (see Chapter 5). Unfortunately we have no precise dates for these changes. As suggested above, the place-name evidence indicates that the creation of a submanor of Bishop's Cleeve could already have occurred by the end of the eighth century when a new lord was settled on the lower slopes of Nottingham Hill slightly away from an existing settlement, bringing slaves to work the land which became his demesne, farmed under his direct control.

This area of Gotherington around the manor-house became known as Upper Gotherington and by Domesday Book comprised a holding of six hides. By this time the Bishop of Worcester had reasserted his direct authority on the main area of settlement which became known as Lower Gotherington, around Cleeve Road and down to Shutter Lane. When did this further division of Gotherington into these two manors take place? It seems possible by the end of the tenth century, for we know that a similar process was occuring on the other side of Bishop's Cleeve, at Southam, where a new manor was created in 991.[7]

The evidence upon which these possibilities have been based is, of course, by no means conclusive. We do not even know whether there were any other small communities living in the area of Gotherington in these years, because the archaeological evidence would be so fragile – timber huts and utensils made from leather and wood leave little or no trace in the ground. Neither do we have any idea of the number of people living here at this time. However, if we know little about the early Anglo-Saxon inhabitants of the area, the various boundary landmarks described in the charters draw a picture for us of how the landscape looked by the eleventh century.

The woodlands which earlier had clothed the valley had been cleared centuries before but woodland still survived on higher ground. Della Hooke in her book describes Bishop's Cleeve as having several names associated with a whole variety of animals which, if not confined to woodland, certainly sought the shelter afforded by heavily wooded regions; names like *Rahlinc* meaning roedeer lynch, *hindlypa* meaning hindleap, *wulflaege*, a wood or clearing frequented by wolves, *rahhege* a roedeer hedge and *heafoc wyllan* a spring frequented by hawks.[8] These names appear on the higher ground of the Cleeve estate. In the vale, cereals were grown and as the enclosed fields of the Romano-British period lost their hedges and fences the landscape gradually took a more open look. The boundary description includes reference to meadow along the streams in the vale.

What did the settlement itself look like? We can only presume that it was similar to other Anglo-Saxon settlements that have been found and excavated. These were really small collections of farms and huts rather than villages. In the earlier Saxon period they shifted location from generation to generation. The houses were built of wood. A house was excavated at Bourton-on-the-Water in the 1930s which was probably very similar to those built in Gotherington. It was part sunk into the ground with a thatched roof, a stone seat and posts for a loom.[9] Oxenton is recorded in Domesday Book as having had a hall or nobleman's house before 1066, but there is no record of one in Gotherington. Although also built of wood these were on a much grander scale like a wooden barn with interior wooden posts in rows to support the large roof and wattle panels covered in daub. In the middle of the floor was an open hearth with the smoke finding its way out through the thatched roof. When the new district offices were being built in Tewkesbury, the site was excavated and the dig revealed the great post socket holes of the great hall of an Anglo-Saxon lord at Tewkesbury.[10] Although there is no mention of a hall at Gotherington in the Domesday Book, this does not mean one did not exist by 1066. It is likely to have been a forerunner of the manor-house in Manor Lane.

THE LIFE OF THE PEOPLE

What was life like for people living in the Gotherington area between 450 and 1086? Carolyn Heighway in her book *Anglo-Saxon Gloucestershire* describes how the Anglo-Saxons developed into a very complex, structured, ordered and close-knit society consisting of noblemen, commoners, freedmen and slaves. No man lived in isolation but was a member of a kindred or family group. If he was killed, custom demanded that his kinsmen avenge his death or secure monetary compensation from his killer's family. The value of the life of a nobleman was 300 shillings; that of a freedman 80, 60 or 40 shillings depending on his status. This sum was paid to the family of the murdered man to buy off the vendetta.

A man needed his kinsmen to swear his innocence if he was accused of a crime. Their number depended on the seriousness of the charge and on their social status. There was little attempt to verify the facts as in a modern court, and the outcome often depended on divine justice. If a man could not find enough people of the right status to swear on oath on his behalf he had to pay a fine or go to the ordeal. The accuser decided the nature of the ordeal. If it was water, the accused was thrown, tied to a rope, into the nearest convenient water, if he floated he was guilty. In the ordeal of hot water he had to snatch a stone from the bottom of a cauldron of boiling water or in the ordeal of iron he had to carry a heated bar a certain distance. He was cleared if his hand showed signs of healing after three days. If this seems unfair to us, to the Saxon mind it allowed the maximum scope for divine intervention.

Justice was administered every four weeks at the hundred court, which every freedman in the village had to attend. The hundred was a subdivision of the shire. It originally comprised a hundred hides. The hundred court for the villagers of Gotherington was held in the open air at the Tibblestone, the origins of which were discussed in Chapter 2. The site of the Tibblestone is characteristic of the ancient sites of many hundred courts. It stood on neutral territory near the boundaries of several parishes equidistant from all those attending the court from their various villages. The choice of a prehistoric standing stone was also quite common. Perhaps it was believed its antiquity gave the court greater authority. By the eleventh century we know that Tibblestone Hundred covered the parishes of Ashton-under-Hill, Beckford, Hinton-on-the-Green, Alstone, Teddington (whose name might be connected with the Tibblestone), Little Washbourne, Bishop's Cleeve, Gotherington, Southam and Brockhampton, Stoke Orchard and Woodmancote. Oxenton and Woolstone were not included. Woolstone had become an outlying part of the Deerhurst Hundred where its justice would have been administered. Oxenton belonged to Tewkesbury and was included in the

The Tibble Stone

The Tibblestone today stands to the south west of the Teddington Hands roundabout

Lower Tewkesbury Hundred.[11] The defining of hundreds gives us another indication of the importance of territories and their boundaries during the Anglo-Saxon period.

Anglo-Saxon society was hierarchical. Most people were peasants supporting by their labour on the land a small aristocracy. The Domesday Book records that a quarter of the population of Gloucestershire were slaves. There were possibly a dozen in Upper Gotherington. The peasants and slaves who lived in Gotherington would nearly all have been farm labourers, including, perhaps bee-keepers, swine and cowherds, wood-wards and hay-wards. The former managed the woodlands and the latter watched grazing animals to keep them out of the crops.

A document dating from towards the end of the Saxon period in the eleventh century called the *Rectitudes* or *Rights and Conditions of Men* describes the work and responsibilities of every class of society. The workload for a peasant was heavy. He had to:

work two days for the lord each week, and three days from February 1st until Easter, pay tithes of ten pence at Michaelmas, and twenty-three sesters of barley and 2 hens at Martinmas, one lamb and two pence at Easter. He had to help with the lambing. At ploughing time he had to supply the seed and plough one acre a week. He had to plough three acres as boon work, two in return for rights of pasturage, three as his tribute land sown from his own seed, and pay his hearth penny. Every two peasants had to maintain a hunting dog and each man gave six loaves to the lord's swineherd when he drove the pigs to pasture in the woods.

In return he was given two oxen, one cow, six sheep and seven acres of land, tools for his work and utensils for his house. When he died the lord took it all back. Even the slaves had a strip of land for raising food and could sell the surplus. It was not unknown for a slave to save up and buy his freedom but whether the slaves in Gotherington bought this freedom or had it granted we do not know, but they disappeared in the century after Domesday. Each family had a piece of land round their cottage for vegetables and herbs and kept a pig. Their diet was monotonous but sustaining, consisting mainly of wholemeal bread and garden vegetables like beans and leeks, fruit in the autumn and whatever game they could hunt on their own land. Most of the utensils used in the home and in the fields were wooden and have not survived, but the most valuable item in all homes was the iron cauldron or cooking pot which would be passed on from generation to generation until it became too patched to be mended.[12] All this comes, of course, from an official document. In reality there was much individual variation. It is also a document from the end of the Saxon period when society had become more organized, but in the absence of more direct evidence it does give us some idea of what life was like for the people of Gotherington before 1066.

Living conditions were very insanitary but probably not as bad in small settlements like Gotherington as they were in the towns like Winchcombe. Everyone had lice and most people had worms. Work done on the skeletons found in the Saxon cemetery of St Oswald's Minster in Gloucester showed that many people suffered from arthritis and some from tuberculosis of the bone. Households were not large; the numbers in each family were similar to those today. Child mortality was not excessively high. A fifth of children died before their first year and perhaps a quarter did not survive their tenth year. Children became adults at twelve. People wore tunics of wool or linen woven at home with patterns or dyed bright colours. They wore cloaks and leggings. When the weather was cold noblemen wore costly furs; the ordinary people wore sheepskins.

Although life consisted of hard physical work there was plenty of opportunity for feasting and merry-making at festivals like Easter, Christmas and the harvest. The *Rectitudes* mention that the lord was obliged to provide winter provisions, Easter provisions, a harvest feast for reaping the corn, a drinking feast for ploughing, reward for haymaking, food for making the rick, at wood-carrying a log from each load, at corn-carrying food on completion of the rick. The highlights of the agricultural year were marked by a great communal feast with the lord providing and everyone joining in.

THE WIDER WORLD

Although the people of Gotherington, like farmers and labourers in every society, were tied to their village and land, they did not live in an isolated community. They were tied to the church at Bishop's Cleeve by tithes, baptisms and burials, and to the court of the Tibblestone Hundred for justice. Winchcombe, a Mercian royal estate centre and venerated royal minster was only six miles away and linked by the route that runs between Nottingham and Dixton Hills and through Gretton. It was the centre of the hereditary land of the princes of the Hwicce, was the place where the Hwiccan family records were kept and was a burial place of the two Mercian princes, King Coenwulf (Kenwulf) and his son Cynhelm (Kenelm). The minster at Winchcombe was founded by Offa of Mercia in 787, or possibly earlier by Hwiccan princes. It was originally a double monastery of monks and nuns but became a house of Benedictine monks by 789. In the eleventh century it enjoyed an era of prosperity and popularity as pilgrims came in great numbers to worship at the tomb of Cynhelm who was believed to be a child martyr, murdered by his wicked stepsister.[13]

Winchcombe increased in importance with the arrival of the Viking invaders at the end of the eighth century. When the Danes made their first raids into English territory the country was disorganized and vulnerable but under the rule of King Alfred of Wessex and his successors it reorganized and slowly pushed the invaders northwards out of the Mercian and Hwiccan kingdoms. This was achieved by fortifying strategic towns including Winchcombe and using them as strong points from which to defend adjacent territory.[14]

Aethelflaed, 'the Lady of the Mercians', the eldest child of Alfred and wife of Earl Ethelred, ruled Mercia from about 902 until 918. She fortified and garrisoned Worcester, Hereford and Gloucester and at about the same time built the defensive walls around Winchcombe. This same campaign saw the organization of shires, each shire being a region that contributed to the military fortification of a single town. Both Gloucester and Winchcombe became shire towns, giving their name to the regions that supported them. Since the reign of Coenwulf (796–821) Bishop's Cleeve, including Gotherington, had been attached to his royal estate at Winchcombe. It now became part of Winchcombeshire which extended eastwards to Adlestrop, southwards to Withington and northwards almost to Stratford-on-Avon.[15] Gotherington like the other shire villages would have been obliged to supply labour to help build and then maintain the Winchcombe fortifications. The earth-bank built in this period still survives along Back Lane on the north-west side of the medieval town. Winchcombe was an important centre with its own mint, market and shops but later during the reign of King Canute (c. 1017), Winchcombeshire was combined with Gloucestershire and it lost its status as a shire.

The Anglo-Saxon period discussed in this chapter lasted over six hundred years. Although it is difficult for us to discover much in detail about what happened, we have been able to sketch a picture which included two small communities on the edge of a large estate based on Bishop's Cleeve, which was created as Roman Britain was transformed into Anglo-Saxon England. The people of Gotherington during these six centuries lived close to the land. Their short, hard lives were spent in a constant struggle to provide food, shelter and clothing for themselves and their lords. Yet their horizons extended beyond their immediate community to the parish of Bishop's Cleeve, the Hundred of Tibblestone, the shires of Winchcombe and Gloucester and to their lord, the Bishop at Worcester.

Life tied to the land changed only slowly, but we have identified two major changes in these years: the restructuring of territories at the end of the Roman period, which brought the area of Gotherington into the estate based on Bishop's Cleeve, then its splitting off, probably by the end of the tenth century. There were changes in the lords who held the lands, but to the peasants, life was still hard and short.

Yet local changes like these must have been far more important for the people at Gotherington than the great events of history. The news that William had defeated Harold at Hastings scarcely affected their lives. It did not help them live longer nor gain their bread more easily. They still had to plough and sow, guard their sheep, cattle and pigs, pay taxes and tithes. Wulstan was still Bishop of Worcester. For the historian, however, the Conquest led to a new monarchy and in 1085 at Gloucester William decided to make an enquiry of his lands. The Domesday Book provides us with some clues about Gotherington at the end of the eleventh century. It forms the basis of the next chapter.

Agricultural worker

References

1   C. Heighway, *Anglo-Saxon Gloucestershire* (Alan Sutton and Gloucestershire County Library, 1987), p. 8.
2   Ibid., p. 18.
3   Ibid., pp. 23–4.
4   For full discussion of the extent and nature of the kingdom of the Hwicce, see D. Hooke, *The Anglo-Saxon Landscape: the Kingdom of the Hwicce* (Manchester University Press, 1985), Chapter 1, pp. 3–23.
5   For this date and the following discussion we are indebted to Dr Steven Bassett, School of History, Birmingham University.
6   The charters, the boundaries and a translation are in G.B. Grundy, *Saxon Charters and Field Names of Gloucestershire*, Part 1 (Bristol and Gloucestershire Archaeological Society, 1935), pp. 71–90.
7   For these ideas we are indebted to Professor Christopher Dyer of Birmingham University. For the subdivision of Southam see H.P.R. Finberg, *Early Charters of the West Midlands* (Leicester University Press, 1972), pp. 63–4, 69.
8   Hooke, op. cit., p. 231.
9   Heighway, op. cit., p. 85.
10 Ibid., p. 86.
11 A.H. Smith, *The Place Names of Gloucestershire*, Vol. II (Cambridge University Press, 1965), pp. 87–9.
12 This description of social life is based on Heighway, op. cit., pp. 77–92.
13 S.R. Bassett, 'A Probable Mercian Royal Mausoleum at Winchcombe, Gloucestershire', *The Antiquaries Journal*, Vol. LXV Part 1, 1985, pp. 81–100.
14 Heighway, op. cit., p. 43.
15 J. Whybra, *A Lost English County: Winchcombeshire in the 10th and 11th Centuries* (Boydell and Brewer, Woodbridge, 1990).

CHAPTER FOUR

'Thurstan, son of Rolf, holds 6 hides in Gotherington'

Gotherington at the Time of Domesday Book, 1086

Bill Spragg

The arrival of the Normans was a comparative ripple to the peasant in Gloucestershire, where there was no rising against the new king with his brutal retaliation as happened in the north of England. There was already a long established exchange across the Channel between the men of power and wealth, and this was the background to William's claim to the English throne. A similar trade and exchange existed with Scandinavia. Communications across the kingdom allowed comparatively easy movement of goods and people, permitting Harold to fight off the Scandinavian attack on the north-east coast, and quickly, but unsuccessfully, attempt the same at Hastings. Twenty years later, those same communications eased the collecting of the survey which covered the whole of England to the present Scottish and Welsh borders and took less than a year to complete. It was only twelve miles away from Gotherington at Gloucester at the Christmas court of 1085, that King William I, after long discussion with his councillors, set in motion the collecting of facts that we call the Domesday Book.

The Domesday Book recorded the late Anglo-Saxon economy of a kingdom bound together by physical communications of road and trackway, which allowed people to travel and trade, and by written communication which distributed the demands and laws of the rulers. The existence of the roads and trackways, and the ease with which they were used is reflected in the speed with which the nationwide survey was completed. In less than twelve months the statistics were collected by four commissioners in Gloucestershire and written out, after checking by further teams of commissioners. People and goods also travelled by ship and boat. For Gloucestershire this meant the busy Severn and Avon bringing trade to Gloucester and Tewkesbury. Gotherington lies only about eight miles from Tewkesbury through which goods not available locally, from coal to herrings, would have been imported. Other goods came through nearer Winchcombe and further Gloucester.

THE DOMESDAY BOOK ENTRY

The entry for Gotherington in the Domesday Book is disappointing. It consists of one line of closely written, abbreviated Latin which reads in translation:

Turstin Fitz Rolf holds 6 hides in Gotherington.

This entry is placed under the Bishop of Worcester's manor of Cleeve for, as we read in the last chapter, Gotherington was a sub-manor, created out of the larger manor of Cleeve. The same thing had happened to Southam and the now lost settlement of *Sapletune* and these three sub-manors were grouped together so we have no means of identifying the individual details relevant to Gotherington. The entry continues to read:

> In these lands there are 8 ploughs in demesne and 22 villeins and 7 bordars with 13 ploughs. There are 20 slaves and 3 pack-horses and a mill rendering 12*d* and a certain amount of meadow.

Even in translation this entry needs further explanation to make good sense. The Domesday commissioners still used the hide as the basis of measurement. The agreed average size by this time seems to have been 120 acres. Villagers (villeins) and smallholders (bordars) were inhabitants of the manorial land who, while they worked for the lord, according to the custom of the area, had land of their own which they and their families cultivated. The slaves and their families belonged to their lord and all their time and energy was devoted to him. The eight ploughs signify the area of land farmed as demesne by the lord of the manor. This was probably about 1,000 acres across the three settlements; peasants – the villeins and bordars – farmed about 1,500 acres. There was a watermill located somewhere in the three settlements which had to pay 12*d* a year to the lord, and some meadow along the streams. It is frustrating that we cannot distil the details for Gotherington from this entry, although some can be identified by working back from later records. The reason for specifying the size of each manor was the tax of six shillings per hide levied by the king each year.

The Domesday Book confirms that Gotherington still lay in Tibblestone Hundred. The lord of the manor has been named as Turstin Fitz Rolf, which can be translated into modern English as Thurstan, son of Rolf. He is thought to have been the standard bearer of Duke William at the Battle of Hastings, and therefore a follower of some standing. Nevertheless, he was treated cautiously by William, as all others of his rank, in that his reward for services rendered came in small parcels of land scattered about the kingdom, so that he could pose no threat by the size and strength of any private army he could easily muster in one place. Thurstan also held land in Gloucestershire at Ampney Crucis, King's Stanley and Coates near Cirencester, Hillesley, Tortworth, Aust and Fretherne east of the Severn; and Alvington west of the Severn.

All the land theoretically belonged to King William, but most was granted to nobles and bishops who in turn granted most of their estates to subtenants. Thurstan was a subtenant of the Bishop of Worcester, but it is unlikely he lived at Gotherington. He enjoyed the profits but probably sublet the manor to a lesser lord living in Upper Gotherington.

THE SOCIAL STRUCTURE

The combined Domesday Book entry for Gotherington, Southam and *Sapletune* indicates a varied social structure of lesser lords, villagers, smallholders and slaves. Some of these lived at Upper Gotherington particularly in the manorial complex of manor-house, church and farm buildings standing above the small planned settlement where the slaves lived. We can be quite certain that the slaves did live here because they became the mondaymen holding half an acre each in 1310. There were probably also one or two scattered farmsteads adjoining the routes to Gretton and Cleeve, where a handful of villagers and smallholders lived. Yet this is not the complete picture of Gotherington in the late eleventh century. A short reference in the Cleeve entry provides a clue that Lower Gotherington, with its farmsteads and houses lying along Cleeve Road and down to Shutter Lane, was not included under Gotherington, but with Cleeve's entry.

The clue refers to a radknight who possessed a holding of a hide with land enough for two ploughs. The next chapter explains how this can be identified with the present Moat Farm in

The trackway through the centre of the settlement of the slaves recorded in the Domesday Book can still be seen between Manor Farm and the railway

Malleson Road. However, that is the only clue we have about this small but separate community, and we have no idea how many people were living there or what sort of people they were. The reason for Lower Gotherington not appearing separately is that it was part of the Bishop of Worcester's greater manor of Cleeve, and was not subtenanted in 1086. The reasons behind this situation were suggested in the previous chapter. Therefore it had no existence separate from Cleeve and no reason for being separately recorded. It serves as a timely reminder to us that the Domesday Book recorded manors, not individual settlements. It cannot be used as gazetteer of places in existence in 1086.

Daily life in Gotherington continued at much the same pace and in the same style as before. At peak periods, like harvest time, the whole family of the villager or smallholder was expected to serve the lord. At other times, as long as the lord's work was done, these families could work on their own farmholdings. The slaves had no choice but to work almost exclusively for their lord. Any freeholders had no labour obligations to the lord at all. Most of the surplus from the villagers' land went to pay tithes, manorial dues and royal taxes, Many of the coins that were used were minted locally. In the earlier years of the Anglo-Saxon period Winchcombe had possessed a mint; by the time of the Domesday Book, Gloucester had become an important centre with four mints known to have existed there.

Although there is no record in Domesday of either the Bishop of Worcester or Thurstan son of Rolf having market rights in Winchcombe, it is more than likely Gotherington people traded there. The extent of the Winchcombe market, because of the size of the borough, would have ensured a good outlet, but added to this would have been the presence of pilgrims. These consumers were on the move throughout the eleventh and into the sixteenth century, making their way to Winchcombe Abbey to the tomb of St Cynhelm. Later in the Middle Ages, after 1250, they might also have been to Hailes Abbey to see the Shrine of the Holy Blood.

AGRICULTURE

We do not possess any direct evidence for agriculture in Gotherington but we can assume it had a typical agrarian economy. The main crops in southern and eastern England were wheat, barley, oats, rye and legumes. Spelt, an inferior species of wheat, continued to be grown in Gloucestershire after it fell out of favour further south and east. Fruit was grown in gardens, together with crops of peas, cabbages, leeks, onions and herbs. The farm tools were mainly made of wood, but they had cutting edges and prongs of metal; they were what we have come to expect of the era – rakes, pitchforks, scythes, flails, riddles and spades. Significantly, the plough underwent an improvement about this period because the mouldboard type made its appearance and this meant that the soil was turned over, creating the ridge-and-furrow pattern in fields that can still be seen in Gotherington today. A plough team usually consisted of eight oxen, but contemporary illustrations sometimes depict fewer.

Meadow was used to produce hay. Horses were recorded in the survey, but there is no mention of goats, pigs, cows and oxen that must also have been kept. They were not recorded because they had no value as a basis for taxation. Cattle were the most common domestic animals throughout this period, but sheep were growing in importance. They appear to have been kept primarily for wool, as is shown by the increasing number that were castrated – an operation which made the fleeces grow more luxuriantly. Domestic pigs were closely related to wild swine, for they were dark and hairy with long legs. They would have fed in the woodlands on the side of Nottingham Hill. Cats and dogs were kept, and domestic fowl. Carts and wagons existed on farms, but interestingly, the Bayeux Tapestry only shows them being pulled by men, and there is no other evidence to show animals harnessed for this purpose.

Salt was still a vital commodity in the eleventh century as it had been in the first century. It was used to help preserve the flesh of animals for the winter. Much meat was also smoked above the perpetual open fires which warmed the houses and provided cooking facilities, but immersing meat in brine, or rubbing in salt before smoking also helped delay the inevitable rotting. Using the salt ways, pack animals or carts brought the precious mineral from far places. The Ordnance Survey map still marks a route running past Hailes up Sudeley Hill as

Mediaeval Mill

Salt Way. No doubt other routes existed to bring salt from Droitwich and Nantwich in Cheshire to Winchcombe. Thereafter it would have been a routine journey that brought the salt from Winchcombe to Gotherington.

The Domesday Book entry includes a mill but we do not know if it was at Gotherington. Windmills had not yet been introduced and it seems unlikely that the mill referred to in the previous chapter lay on the Gotherington side of the boundary with Woolstone. The lord had exclusive rights to milling and gained a profit from his tenants. The remains of hand querns found in other places suggest not every villager was happy with this official situation.

Upper Gotherington was a sub-manor of Bishop's Cleeve, but the whole of Gotherington was dependent upon Cleeve for church ritual. This, of course, dated back to the eighth century at least. It is interesting to compare the Domesday entry for Bishop's Cleeve with that of Gotherington. It reads:

> There are 30 hides, 3 ploughs in demesne, 16 villagers and 19 smallholders with 16 ploughs. There are 8 slaves and 1 horse. A priest has 1 hide and 2 ploughs. A radknight with 1 hide and 2 ploughs. There is a very small wood.

There are slightly fewer villagers, many more smallholders but fewer slaves than the entry of which Gotherington is part. The area of arable land was approximately the same. A priest is recorded because he held a sub-manor from the bishop, which was probably created to provide income for the church when the estate passed to the Bishop of Worcester before 899 after the failure of the minster. The radknight is the clue that Lower Gotherington lay in this manor. The wood is Bushcombe Wood (Bushcombe means 'the bishop's valley') on Nottingham Hill.

Other entries in the Domesday Book throw some possible light on the duties of the radknight. His main duty was to provide a messenger for the bishop, but he had other duties. These might have included working either on or off the estate, supplying transport, and driving herds. The radknights who lived in the manors around Tewkesbury 'ploughed and harrowed at their lord's court', and those living on Deerhurst manor, including Pamington and Tredington, 'harrowed, scythed and reaped for the use of the lord' while they also had lands, ploughs and dependants of their own. The radknight at Bishop's Cleeve had a sizeable holding which would have had people to work on it, but they are not recorded in the Domesday Book because they created wealth for the radknight and not the bishop. For such reasons the Domesday Book cannot be used as a guide to the total population of any place, even if we assume the people recorded represented families not just individuals.

LAW AND ORDER

There was no speedy change after the Conquest. The shire court met twice a year and was attended by the earl or sheriff, the bishops and theigns representing the towns and hundreds. The hundred court continued to meet every month at the Tibblestone and was attended by men from Gotherington and the other townships in the hundred. King William was very firm on law and order in his new kingdom. He introduced exact fines for a variety of offences of civil disobedience and dishonesty. Anyone giving false measure was fined 4*d*; making bad beer meant punishment with the dung stool; allowing a fire to spread meant a fine of 3 ora (this is a unit of weight of Scandinavian origin) of pence, with an extra 2*d* paid to the neighbours. For offences against property there were no half measures. A fine of 100*s* was levied for highway robbery, for housebreaking, and for violence to women. For the crime of bloodshed, the penalty was dependent upon when the crime was committed. For example, in neighbouring Worcestershire 'Whoever shed blood between Monday morning and Saturday noon was fined 10*s*.' But from Saturday noon to Monday morning, the fine was 20*s*, as it was for the twelve days of Christmas and the first day of Easter. Whoever killed a man on these holy days was fined £4, and on other days 40s. The accused's chances of acquittal depended on the successful production of 'witnesses', not the careful weighing of evidence as happens today. The system described in the last chapter was still in existence.

The impression we gain from Domesday Book is of a male dominated society. No women are specifically mentioned in Gotherington although it is possible some of the villagers or smallholders were female, probably widows holding land in their own right. Female slaves are usually recorded and there were none recorded in Gotherington. Women do appear in the Domesday Book and some are named as landowners. Edeva the Fair held a number of manors in Lancashire; Golde and her son had three hides in Huntingdonshire, while 'Angar's woman, a widow, . . . held 2 hides as a manor in Hertfordshire'. But the overall impression from the Domesday Book is that few women were in control of land, however large or small the holding. However, there is ample evidence from the time of the Domesday Book that the general attitude towards women was one of affection and caring, witnessed by these two extracts from nearby Worcestershire: 'Wulfin who lay ailing, made sure that his friends and priest heard his wish that his wife should hold his land for as long as she lived, and only then would the land return to the church'; 'When he [Sigref] died, the bishop gave his daughter, with this land, to one of his men-at-arms,' so that 'he might maintain [her] mother and serve the bishop'.

At the time of the Conquest, slavery was an accepted practice. The slave was a chattel, and in law, although perhaps not in fact, he had no family. If he was killed, a few pence might be given to his family, but the bulk of the recompense went to his master. The slave did, however, have some entitlements: the *Rectitudes* tell us: 'Every slave ought to have provisions of twelve pounds of good corn and two carcases of sheep and one good cow for food and the right of cutting wood according to the custom of the estate'. He received extra food at Christmas and Easter and a strip of land for ploughing or, if he were a herdsman, a young pig in a sty.

The count of slaves in Gloucestershire was more than two thousand, nearly a quarter of the recorded population – a very high proportion compared to the rest of the country. In Bristol the slave market did a good business in exporting slaves to Ireland. However, slavery did not long outlast the Conquest. The king attempted to stop it and Bishop Wulstan brought slavery to an end in his diocese of Worcester. In Gotherington the slaves at Domesday became the mondaymen of the thirteenth century. They will be discussed in the next chapter.

It is perhaps necessary to reiterate that in the turmoil that followed William's victory at Hastings, the daily and seasonal routine that ticked over in Gotherington appears hardly to have been disturbed. Villagers may have seen new faces and figures at the manor-house, but with all the widespread possessions of Thurstan, son of Rolf, he would only have visited occasionally, if at all. Trade and other contacts with the neighbouring villages, particularly Bishop's Cleeve, continued, with occasional longer journeys to Winchcombe, Tewkesbury and Gloucester.

The Domesday Book provides us with a fragmentary snapshot of the settlement at a time of change. Relationships between lords and peasants were being formalized; the landscape was being, or had recently been, transformed into one which can be recreated from the present landscape. Increasingly such changes can be traced from the written word which becomes more available after 1086. They form the basis of the next chapter which brings the story of Gotherington nearer to our own day.

References

This chapter has been compiled from the following sources:

1   T. Hinde, *The Domesday Book* (Alecto Historical Editions, Guild Publishing, London).
2   O.G. Tomkeieff, *Life in Norman England* (Batsford, London).
3   D. Butler, *1066 – The Story of a Year* (Anthony Bload).
4   J. Sawyer, *The Story of Gloucestershire* (Norman, Sawyer and Co., Cheltenham).

CHAPTER FIVE

Bishops and Abbots

The Story of Gotherington in the Later Middle Ages

David Aldred

This chapter traces the history of Gotherington from the Domesday Book to the early 1500s. For the first time we are able to examine the area in some detail. We learn the names of some of the inhabitants, discovering where some of them lived and what work they did. The picture becomes clearer because an increasing amount of evidence survives. We still possess a handful of manorial surveys between *c.* 1170 and *c.* 1540, a list of tax-payers of 1327, and a collection of court cases between 1412 and 1514. They will be used not only as snapshots of Gotherington at particular times, but also to identify some of the changes and continuities within this period. Yet we must not forget these are the records of the people who ruled over the peasants of Gotherington, who are only really heard when their lords allowed. The evidence for their lives has to be found in the landscape itself, and the chapter ends by examining how much of their handiwork survived into modern times.

The documents tell us that the manorial distinctions between Upper and Lower Gotherington continued into the sixteenth century and later. There continued to be significant differences both in the nature of landholding and the type of peasant living there, although their lives were inextricably intertwined. We start this chapter by examining the people who were the landholders.

THE LANDHOLDERS

The continuing integrity of Thurstan's six hide Domesday holding at Upper Gotherington does provide an important thread for the historian to follow throughout this period. Thurstan himself did not remain lord for very long after 1086. By *c.* 1100 the Bishop of Worcester had granted the holding to another sub-tenant, Winebald de Ballon. Some historians think Winebald gained his lands because he had supported King William Rufus on his campaigns into Wales.[1]

By 1166 Upper Gotherington had passed to his grandson, Henry of Newmarket, who was holding it at the time of the survey of the bishop's lands *c.* 1170, when he had to provide the bishop with support for half a knight if the king demanded it, just like the previous holders back to Saxon times.[2] Possibly to fulfil this obligation Henry had already granted the manor to Hugh Bigod, the first Earl of Norfolk, whose main lands lay in far away East Anglia.[3] When Hugh died in 1176, Upper Gotherington passed via his wife Gundreda to his son Roger, who became involved in the unrest during the reign of King John. He was imprisoned in 1213 but redeemed after the monks of Tewkesbury Abbey had paid eighty-four silver marks (£56) and two palfreys to the king. It seems that it was in gratitude that Roger granted them Upper Gotherington in 1220 in return for an annual payment of 12*d* twice a year

The present appearance of Manor Farm gives no indication that this is the site of the medieval manor complex of Upper Gotherington. The dovecot on the left could well be built of the stones from the chapel-of-ease which is known to have existed there until the seventeenth century

to him and his heirs in order to acknowledge a continuing theoretical overlordship.[4]

We know King John was a generous benefactor of Tewkesbury and its abbey, but whether or how this affected the events we do not know. Certainly Upper Gotherington must have been an inconvenient outlying manor for Roger Bigod.[5] Nevertheless this did not prevent Roger's brother Richard trying to claim back the manor from the abbey in 1221, in which attempt he failed. The monks of Tewkesbury did not administer the manor directly because they had installed their own sub-tenant and were content to receive a modest annual profit of half a mark (6s 8d) which spared them the inconvenience of running the manor themselves.[6] It is, of course, quite possible the same sub-tenant had been there during the time of the Bigods' overlordship. We just do not know. However, these events serve as a reminder that people who held land in late medieval Gotherington did not live there. Nevertheless, the Bigods continued to be identified with Upper Gotherington. In 1260 a Henry Bigod and his wife Margery were recorded as living in the community; they were possibly a minor branch of the family, installed in the manor-house as the sub-tenants. In 1535 the Abbot of Tewkesbury was still paying the Bishop of Worcester 10d each year for 'land once Bigods' .[7]

During the four and a half centuries under consideration here, we only know with certainty the names of two sub-tenants who held Upper Gotherington from the abbot. The first was Almaric of St Amand who died in 1310. He paid the abbot 2s each year but kept the profits of the manor totalling £11 13s 11d for himself. The survey, or inquisition, taken at his death provides us with valuable details about the settlement and we shall investigate it below.[8] The second sub-tenant was Richard Weller who farmed (i.e. rented) the manor site and its lands from 1517. He paid the monks £8 8s annually and kept the holding when the abbey was dissolved in 1540.[8] Unlike Almaric (whose main holdings lay in Ireland) he actually lived in the manor-house.[9]

The bishop, the abbot, the Bigods, Almaric of St Amand and Richard Weller held Upper Gotherington for the wealth they hoped it would bring them. The peasants toiled to create it. The successors to the Domesday slaves continued to live beneath the manor-house complex. A kilometre away to the west the farms of the unfree tenants mingled into those of the free tenants of Lower Gotherington in what is now the village centre. How was the land held in this other manor of Lower Gotherington?

We read in the last chapter how Lower Gotherington appeared hidden within the Domesday Book entry for Bishop's Cleeve. Not until the survey of the Bishop of Worcester's estates taken *c*. 1170 do we gain any detailed information about its nature.[10] The picture that emerges here and which continues, is of the bishop maintaining his lordship over a community comprising a small number of free tenants who held larger than average holdings in return for money rents and a variety of services to the bishop. They were five in number in *c*. 1170. The 1299 survey records an additional six tenants holding smaller holdings but with heavier and more specific services to the bishop. It was very different, therefore, from Upper Gotherington which was much larger and inhabited by unfree tenants, tied more closely to the lord's demands.

Chief of the tenants in Lower Gotherington in status, if not in size of holding, were those who held land by military service, together providing half the upkeep of a knight; this was part of the obligation laid down on the whole of Gotherington at the time of the separation from Bishop's Cleeve possibly as early as the eighth century. The Earls of Gloucester held land by this service in both *c*. 1170 and 1299. At the earlier date it was sub-tenanted by Alexander; in 1299 by John the Barber. Robert Young also held by a share in this service. He had a large holding of seven yardlands, about two hundred acres in *c*. 1170. This had been subdivided into three by 1299. In *c*. 1170 there were another three holdings; by 1299 there were six. The

At the rear of Moat Farm a small section of the medieval moat still exists

White's Farm was one of the freeholdings of Lower Gotherington. It has changed little since this picture was taken earlier in the twentieth century when the milk churn betrayed its function as a dairy farm

largest and most interesting of these was the one which came into the hands of the Pendock family by 1290. It was a hide in extent (120 acres) and was held by paying the Bishop of Worcester 13s 4d annually. It remained in the Pendock family for over three hundred years and can be identified with Moat Farm. The building of a fashionable moated house, possibly in the fourteenth century, was a sure sign the Pendocks had aspirations to being quasi-lords of the manor, although their main landholding continued to be across the Severn at Pendock in Worcestershire. Significantly by 1475 they were alone responsible for providing for a knight and enjoyed a high status in the community. Of the other four holdings recorded c. 1170 it is very likely that three of them are represented today by Home Farm, Hales Farm and White's Farm, although which was which is impossible now to discover.

We do not know how much time the Pendocks and the other free tenants actually spent living in Gotherington. Robert Francis, a free tenant recorded c. 1170, had a house in Southam, 90 acres of land in Woodmancote and 120 acres in Cleeve itself. His half hide holding in Lower Gotherington was in the hands of someone called Gerold, so Robert probably remained an absentee sub-tenant of the bishop.[11] In 1450 the heirs of William Chaumond who had held one and a half yardlands (forty-five acres) in 1299, were living in Cheltenham and Gloucester.[12] On the other hand signatures and seals appended to grants of land do indicate even absentee landlords must have visited their holdings at least on occasion.[13]

The handful of freeholders were the real 'lords' of Lower Gotherington. They enjoyed freedom from working for the bishop; they dealt in land; they hired labourers to work their fields; they were looked up to by the less free villagers around them, several of whom tried to join them by commuting or changing their labour services to the bishop into money. Yet they were not real lords and they were still subject to the custom of the bishop's manor. When Thomas Pendock died in 1413, the bishop took two oxen worth 30s for his heriot (i.e. payment on death) and his son William had to pay 14s 8d to regain the family holding.[14] Three generations later in 1525, Richard and William Pendock were fined a total of 18d for making a dunghill in the road at Upper Gotherington.[15] Nevertheless, they enjoyed freedoms and status far above those of the ordinary villagers.

Who Were the Villagers?

In this section the manors of Upper and Lower Gotherington will be considered individually and then the links between them will be examined. We will start by considering how many people lived in the two settlements.

We have read already how the Domesday Book cannot be used for this purpose, and so the best starting point for Upper Gotherington comes from the other end of the period. It is provided by two surveys conducted in 1540 and 1555 after the dissolution of Tewkesbury Abbey.[16] They both contain twenty-six names so we can assume twenty-six families, but both surveys indicate the population had been larger, for some tenants had double, triple or even quadruple holdings, and there are references to tofts and closes – the gardens and paddocks within which houses and barns once stood, but which lay empty and deserted by the time of the surveys. If we assume all these empty properties once held farmsteads, the maximum size of Upper Gotherington was around forty-five families, perhaps between 200 and 250 people – a sizeable community. This peak is likely to have been reached in the early fourteenth century before a series of bad harvests and the Black Death of 1348–9 reduced the population, perhaps by a half or a third. We have two records which give numbers of people for these years.

The description of the settlement given in the inquisition after the death of Almaric of St Amand in 1310 lists twenty-seven families besides Almaric's own. The near contemporary general taxation, or lay subsidy, of 1327 lists all Gotherington tax-payers in one entry. We can work out that probably twenty-one of them were living at Upper Gotherington.[17] The usual rate of evasion and exemption is thought by historians to be about 60 per cent. This would give a total of fifty families. Even if the rate of evasion and exemption was not so high, the total is much closer to that worked back from the sixteenth century, than the number suggested for 1310. The most likely explanation for the discrepancy is that the inquisition tended to underrecord the population, a not unusual occurrence. Yet even these might have been underestimated, for in 1555 some tenants were accused of keeping their own under-tenants 'against the custom of the manor'.[18] They would have been paid to do the work of the tenants. All the evidence suggests the population of Upper Gotherington grew to a maximum of around 250 people in the early and mid-fourteenth century, when it contracted, and by the mid-sixteenth century numbered around 150. A dozen families lived below the manor-house; from the four holdings which can be identified (see Chapter 7) the rest lay crammed along Cleeve Road and Gretton Road. What was life like for these people?

To answer this question we can start with the inquisition into the holding of Almaric of St Amand taken at his death in 1310 and already used to help work out the population. It describes how the manor-house stood in a garden with two dovecots. Almaric's demesne, the land not rented out to the tenants, totalled 240 acres of arable land scattered throughout the open fields; eight acres of meadow; and about fifteen acres of pasture, presumably on the slopes above the manor-house. There was some meadow along the Tyrl Brook to the north, but we know some meadow attached to Gotherington was located at Oxenton and in Cleeve meadow at Bredon in 1555, and this could well have been the case in 1310, for suitable land for growing hay was very scarce within Gotherington's boundaries.[19]

Almaric took 10s annual profit from his windmill to which all his tenants should have taken their grain for grinding to flour. This stood on the elevated part of the field off Manor Lane to the west of the railway line. Two free tenants on the manor paid him 2s each year on the feast of St Cynhelm (17 June), the boy martyr whose body lay in Winchcombe Abbey. These two tenants had large holdings – 120 acres between them. One of these holdings can be identified with the present Baldwin's Farm. This high acreage and low rental put them in a doubly favourable position compared to the rest of the peasants at Upper Gotherington who owed heavy labour services and very little land. Twelve of them were called natives, indicating their unfree status. They held half a yardland each. From 29 September to 24 June they worked two

Baldwin's Farm was one of the two freeholdings of Upper Gotherington

days each week on Almaric's land. From 24 June to 1 August the demands of the hay harvest added another day each week. A day's work was valued at ½d. From 1 August to 29 September the demands of the grain harvest lifted the value of each day's work to 1d. On 29 September these peasants had to spend the day ploughing on the lord's demesne. Only when the lord's demands had been satisfied could they work on their own land.

After the natives were listed the thirteen villeins, holding an acre of land each, i.e. the toft or croft on which their house stood. We would not usually expect to find the term 'villein' for such smallholders. They were the successors to the Domesday slaves, working for Almaric one day a week throughout the year, worth ½d per day except at harvest when it was worth 1d. They provided a ready supply of hired labour for the half-yardlanders and larger landholders in both Upper and Lower Gotherington. Their timber-framed houses stood in the planned settlement beneath the manor-house. It was the natives who lived further away from the manor along the roads to Bishop's Cleeve and Gretton. Together with the two free tenants they lived away from the controlling influence of the manor-house. The total area of arable land attached to the manor was 563 acres. This was scattered throughout all the fields of Gotherington, for the distinction into two manors was administrative rather than obviously geographical. Nevertheless, at the two extremes of the settlement, among the freehold farms in modern Malleson Road and among the servile tenants around the manor-house, Lower and Upper Gotherington were distinct. How did life in Lower Gotherington contrast with that of its neighbour?

We have to estimate the size of its population from the surveys of c. 1170, 1299 and c. 1475, and the lay subsidy of 1327.[20] A major problem in trying to do this is that we cannot be absolutely certain how many people listed actually lived in Lower Gotherington. We have already read how some landholders, for example, the Pendock family, had property elsewhere. In 1327 the rector of Bishop's Cleeve is recorded in the Gotherington entry because he had wealth there, possibly sheep, not because he lived there. However, the figures we do possess from these four records give five villagers c. 1170; fourteen in 1299; nine, including the rector of Bishop's Cleeve, in 1327; and six in c. 1475. If we assume 60 per cent evasion and exemption in 1327, there were twenty families in Lower Gotherington at that date. As with the figure for Upper Gotherington this could be a slight overestimate and the figure of fourteen tenants of 1299, which is likely to have meant fourteen holdings, whether or not the people named in the survey lived in the community, gives an indication of the maximum size of Lower Gotherington before the fourteenth century decline in population. As a manor it was smaller than Upper Gotherington, but the tenants were freer people. We can see this most clearly in the 1299 survey.

The people recorded at Lower Gotherington all enjoyed considerable freedoms when compared with those in Upper Gotherington. Richard Bury held half a yardland for 3s 4d. His father had paid the bishop a sum of money to be freed from his labour services, but this had not made him free because as the survey notes he could not allow his son or daughter to leave the manor without the bishop's permission. John Beadle also held half a yardland for 4s but did not have to pay this when he acted as the beadle, summoning people when the bishop came. Hugh Smith was another half-yardlander whose payment and labour services at harvest were annulled by making parts for ploughs. The survey then records two free tenants each holding only six acres and a house. Thomas Levett was excused his 3s payment by keeping the lord's pigs. William de Sollers had entered into an agreement with the bishop to keep the holding for the same sum. His main holding lay over the Nottingham Hill at Postlip. In 1287 he had been granted land in Bishop's Cleeve as reward for acting as the bishop's groom.[21] It is most unlikely he lived in Gotherington; he would have enjoyed the incomes from the rent paid by a sub-tenant. Only one tenant in the 1299 survey clearly still carried out labour services for the lord. Richard Cook held a house and garden for 12d and had to provide assistance with one man at harvest. In return he was to receive three sheaves of corn.

The names and obligations of these six tenants are also indications of the more varied social structure of Lower Gotherington compared to Upper Gotherington. The beadle, smith, cook and swineherd were tied in their duties to the centre of the manor, at Bishop's Cleeve itself, particularly when the bishop was visiting. William de Sollers was a known 'foreigner'; the Bury family was trying to buy its freedom from the lord. Through the uncertainties of the records the picture that emerges is that the manors did have significant differences in the type of families living in them. However, these were legal distinctions and overall the two manors formed a continuous settlement. What similarities, therefore, did the two manors possess?

In daily life the people of Gotherington intermingled as part of one straggling settlement. Both communities shared a common dependence upon agriculture, villagers in both communities owed labour services to an absentee lord, and both communities were responsible for good order under the authority of the Bishop of Worcester's court. Their strips of arable land lay intermixed in the open fields of the vale. Their animals grazed together on the pasture on Nottingham Hill and the stone from quarries on the hill was used by them all. Their houses continued to look very similar: straw thatched, cruck-framed longhouses open to the roof with family and animals living at opposite ends. By the early thirteenth century some would have been rebuilt on low stone walls to preserve better the bottom timbers. By 1350 house and byre had been separated so that a small collection of farm buildings including barn, pigsty and henhouse stood together around a farmyard. This formed the messuage. The villagers had to keep their buildings in good repair and the houses of the richer tenants were the forerunners of some of the timber-framed houses standing in the village today.

On both manors the villagers increased their independence from their lord as the centuries passed. Even in Upper Gotherington their labour services were being replaced by cash payments, and the last reference to labour services is found in the rental of c. 1475. As the feudal ties lessened, some villagers attempted to claim they were free tenants. John Hathaway

A medieval plough-team based upon a drawing in the Luttrell Psalter

of Upper Gotherington was accused in court of doing this in 1461 and again in 1469.[22] Unfortunately we do not know the outcome. The site of his holding is marked on the map on page 60. Such evidence clearly suggests life was improving for the villagers between 1086 and the early 1500s, but what exactly was it like to live in Gotherington six or seven hundred years ago?

In a recent book Professor Christopher Dyer of Birmingham University has painted a picture of the peasantry in Bishop's Cleeve in the years around 1300.[23] We can assume that his picture also holds good for the peasants of Gotherington, many of whom lived under the same influence of the Bishop of Worcester and held similar holdings to those in Cleeve itself.

The most favoured peasants were those who held a yardland or more, i.e. seven free tenants in Lower and two in Upper Gotherington in 1299. They had sufficient land to grow grain to feed themselves and their animals and still have a small cash surplus to pay rents and dues, hire

The rebuilding of Shady Nook in Shutter Lane exposed its cruck construction, suggesting a fifteenth-century date which might link it to one of the small freeholdings of Lower Gotherington recorded in 1299

labourers and pay royal taxes. In any one year half their holding was cultivated and the other half left fallow. Typical crops were barley, wheat, and peas and oats in a ratio 3:2:1. The wheat, barley and oats made the staple food, pottage. Some barley provided ale. After the rector took his tithe (tenth) and the miller his twenty-fourth, the surplus was sold for cash to add to the sale of animals. Typical livestock were a couple of oxen, a couple of cows, thirty sheep and a pig, pastured on the fallow land to restore its fertility, and on Nottingham Hill pasture. Calves and lambs were used as replacements or sold, wool was sold and surplus cheese was sold, possibly in the markets at Cheltenham, Tewkesbury or Winchcombe. The pig was eaten. Small amounts of income also came from the sale of eggs, honey, perhaps flax and hemp, and the wife's work, typically brewing and spinning yarn.

Income had to be balanced against expenditure. Taxes and rents had to be paid, labourers hired at harvest and ploughing, house repairs and tools paid for, and replacement furniture and clothing bought. In most years the free tenants had a cushion against hard times, but it could soon disappear. In the early 1290s there were bad harvests, sheep disease in the wet summers, and the royal tax in 1327 cost the equivalent of the price of two sheep. Across the Bishop of Worcester's estates in the West Midlands 10 to 15 per cent of tenants died in the famine years 1315–18. In the whole of Cleeve manor, including Lower Gotherington, the number of tenants fell from ninety-four in 1299 to sixty-one in 1349 at the time of the Black Death, a reduction of a third, and it is unlikely that free tenants were immune from this drop.

Even without these external influences, poverty and hardship were part of the regular cycle of life. On the death of a tenant the bishop or abbot took the best beast, the rector the second best, and even if his widow or son inherited, a payment (called an entry fine) had to be made before they could take over the holding. These outgoings were substantial, and likely to plunge the new tenant into debt for several years as he or she tried to build up the animal stock and possibly put the buildings into good shape. Young children demanded food and time but added nothing to the family income. As they grew up this situation changed, but their parents were likely to meet chronic poverty again in their old age as labour had to be hired to work the holding or they added to the burdens of their children with young families by surrendering their holding and going to live with them. Many of course never reached this stage. Nevertheless free tenants enjoyed a privileged position, so how did the unfree tenants survive?

As Professor Dyer points out, it is not at all clear how they did manage to survive. The half-yardlanders in Lower Gotherington were better off than those in Upper Gotherington because they paid their dues in cash or in special service – beadle, smith or cook – which was probably worth 10s compared to the economy of the customary half-yardlanders in Upper Gotherington, but even they must have struggled. Crops were only grown on half their holding in each year. They would only just have fed the family, paid the tithes and milling tolls. Profits from the sale of animals were less because their total numbers were probably only half those of the free tenants. Profits from the garden, poultry and earnings of the wife and children had heightened importance. The tax demand of 1327 was comparatively more harsh than on the free tenants, so too were the heriot, mortuary dues and entry fines. Most half-yardlanders would have lived in debt and sought paid work to help them balance their budgets.

In 1310 there were thirteen tenants in Upper Gotherington who held just one acre each. Although their labour services took only one day out of each week, their plot grew only a small part of their needs. The family had to buy or barter with neighbours for most of what it required. The sale of poultry, yarn and honey probably provided some income but to survive the family needed paid work as labourers, competing with half-yardlanders. They would have worked for wages on the Abbot of Tewkesbury's demesne which totalled 240 acres, unlike their ancestors who worked on it as slaves. The two free tenants in Upper Gotherington held 360 acres between them and this would have provided more opportunities. In Lower Gotherington a similar area was also held by the free tenants and work was available there. This situation reminds us again that the two manors made one community.

CHANGE

This picture of life in Gotherington was not static. There were many changes, both major and minor during the later Middle Ages. One of the most important changes in Upper Gotherington was the break-up of the demesne land and its division among the villagers. We have no evidence for the timescale of this development, except it was complete by 1497.[24] Only a few small plots of meadow and pasture remained attached to the manor-house when Richard Weller began to rent it in 1517.[25] By 1500 there was too much arable land for the population of Upper Gotherington, for many of the strips in the open fields were laid to permanent pasture. When William Steward took a lease on a half yardland holding in 1508, three of the fifteen acres had been put down to permanent pasture – a not untypical ratio.[26] By this date also, small enclosed fields had been created enclosing furlongs (i.e. groups) of ridges and furrows on the lower slopes of Nottingham Hill and they too had been put down to pasture.

With the fall in population in the mid-fourteenth century and the break-up of the demesne, the holdings in Upper Gotherington lost their standard sizes. By 1540 some very large holdings had emerged. The largest was that of Thomas Hughes who held fifty-four acres of arable in the open fields. These gave him rights to pasture fifteen horses or oxen and forty sheep on Nottingham Hill and on the fallow; very necessary to keep the land fertile. He no longer carried out labour services, instead he made an annual payment of Richard Weller of 36s 4½d. Four other villagers had built up holdings of over fifty acres. Ten of the twenty-one tenants had holdings larger than the customary half yardland of fifteen acres and only one still held a single acre.[27]

The medieval ridge and furrow survives to its greatest extent on the lower slopes of Nottingham Hill where it has been put to pasture and not ploughed out as it has been in the vale

When holdings were added together, the buildings attached to one of them were likely to become superfluous, particularly the dwelling. In 1469 John Hathaway stood accused in the bishop's court of demolishing a house and granary.[28] He was obviously an awkward tenant for we met him earlier in the chapter trying to establish himself as a free tenant. This is evidence that the tenants of Upper Gotherington were becoming more like the freeholders of Lower Gotherington, with larger holdings and lessening labour services. The settlement was becoming more homogeneous.

THE OUTSIDE WORLD

Many of the links with the outside world described earlier continued. Villagers went to Bishop's Cleeve to the bishop's court and to church; to Cheltenham and Winchcombe to market; to Gloucester and Tewkesbury for goods brought by river; to Worcester and Tewkesbury to attend their lord's courts.

Although many families lived in Gotherington over several generations, others came and went. It is almost impossible to trace any of this movement, except for those men who joined the church. In the Bishop of Worcester's registers several priests carried the surname 'Gotherington' and so we can presume that they originated from here. Walter was ordained priest in Worcester in 1289; Richard ordained deacon in 1305, probably in London. In 1320 William, rector of Dry Marston near Stratford, died; in 1328 Reginald was recorded as rector of Aldington in Kent; in 1375 another William was made rector of Tirley. He died in 1394 when a Brother John was recorded as a monk at Tewkesbury Abbey.[29]

THE CHURCH

Six men entering holy orders in less than a century from two communities does not necessarily indicate the people of Gotherington were any more religious than people in other communities; but in an age of harsh uncertainty religious faith was probably of greater significance than today. The annals of Tewkesbury Abbey in fact record a miracle of restored sight to a peasant called Richard of Gotherington on St Swithin's day in 1232.[30] Everybody had to attend Bishop's Cleeve church for baptisms, marriages and burials. The villagers of Lower Gotherington had to attend for their Sunday and holy day worship but those of Upper Gotherington had their own chapel-of-ease at the manor, now long gone.[31]

The church had significance greater than its influence on personal beliefs and behaviour. As an institution it affected every part of people's lives. It gave them their holy days of rest and recreation, it demanded tithes and other dues, it regulated community life and, most important of all, was the landlord from which each villager held his or her land.

Some of the records of the Bishop of Worcester's court held at Bishop's Cleeve survive from between the years 1412 to 1514. They provide us with a record of law and order in Gotherington, and the picture they paint suggests the people of the two manors enjoyed basically good order while experiencing the trials and tribulations common to any community. The villagers themselves still had the basic responsibility for administering justice when it appeared to have broken down, but judgements were now passed in the court of the lord, not in the open at the Tibblestone by the community itself.

One of the commonest transgressions was failing to turn up to the court itself. By 1412 the Abbot of Tewkesbury regularly paid the two shillings to be excused attending the court.[32] By the middle of the century the two largest tenants in Lower Gotherington, John Pygas and Robert Pendock, had followed his example, thus providing further evidence for the weakening of the feudal bonds.[33] The commonest criminal allegation was against the miller who was constantly brought before the court accused of taking more than his customary

The sign Church Walk is a reminder of the direct way from
Gotherington to the parish church in Bishop's Cleeve

twenty-fourth part of the grain. In 1414 he was fined 4*d* for the offence – no doubt a small
price to pay for an occupational fiddle.[34] Another common crime was the brewing of
unlicensed ale which thus deprived the bishop of a small income. This was typically a female
occupation. It was rife in Upper Gotherington: eleven people were fined in 1413 and twelve
during the following year.[35] Significantly no one from the comparatively richer families of
Lower Gotherington was ever accused of the offence. If the court records are an accurate
reflection of the situation, they confirm the need of the villagers of Upper Gotherington to
seek alternative income to that from their inadequate plots of land. Violent crime, on the
other hand, was rare. In 1413 Richard Swallow 'drew blood unjustly' from David Welshman
and was fined 6*d*.[36] In 1469 Richard Canty attacked Richard Pendock using a fork and then a
billhook. He was fined the same amount and the weapons were confiscated.[37] We can only
speculate whether these were personal feuds or the result of underlying social tensions, but
only two incidents over a century suggests Gotherington was generally a law abiding place.

In the four and a half centuries after the Domesday Book, the temporal and spiritual power
of the church rested heavily on the villagers of Gotherington; bishop and abbot controlled
their lives. Those lives were always hard and often short. They were tied to the seasons of the
year and if the villagers did move out of Gotherington, temporarily to market in
Winchcombe, or permanently to live on another manor, they could not easily escape the dues
and services they had to pay to their lords.

Thus far this chapter has been based on the written records produced by the lords. If we
seek the legacy of the peasants themselves, we must read it in the landscape. Fossilized in the
fields around the modern village lies much of the late medieval landscape of Gotherington.
This forms the subject for the last part of this chapter.

THE LATE MEDIEVAL LANDSCAPE

The map overleaf is an attempt to recreate the late medieval landscape at its greatest extent. It
has been based on fieldwalking and a study of aerial photographs, taken shortly after the

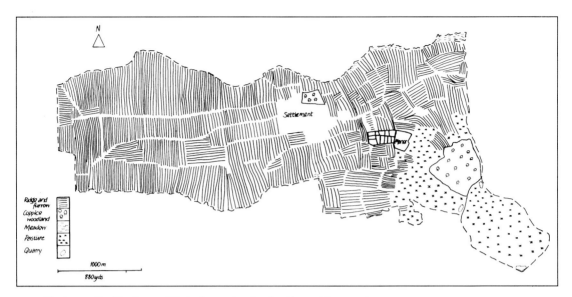

The late medieval landscape of Gotherington showing the ridge and furrow at its greatest extent

Second World War before modern agricultural techniques destroyed much of the corrugated ridge-and-furrow pattern of the medieval open fields.[38] Each tenant had a number of strips, which comprised one or more adjacent ridges, according to the amount of land he or she held. The corrugated effect seems to have been created by the action of the medieval plough.

The ridge and furrow dominates the landscape from the flat land of the vale onto the lower slopes of Nottingham Hill – a sure sign of population pressure before the early fourteenth century. Evidence for this happening between *c.* 1170 and 1299 can be found in these two surveys. In Lower Gotherington *c.* 1170 there were recorded eleven yardlands of agricultural land; in 1299 fourteen and a half. The lines on the map have been drawn at approximately one line for every two ridges on the ground. They are regularly laid out across most of the area they cover which suggests they were planned at some stage. This is likely to have been when, possibly in the late tenth century, Gotherington was separated from Bishop's Cleeve. Unfortunately it is impossible to identify which strips were part of Upper or Lower Gotherington. Every available surface was taken in the vale, which caused problems for other necessary land uses, especially meadow, which was confined to tiny plots along the Tyrl to the north. Grazing on the slopes of Nottingham Hill came under pressure as the arable land encroached onto it as the population grew. Here the small and irregular blocks of ridge and furrow provide clear evidence of this later change: the longer established ridges are much longer and more regular, particularly in the vale. There is nothing unusual in such an extensive spread of the ridge and furrow in the settlements at the foot of the Cotswold scarp. The same pattern can be seen in Gotherington's neighbours at Woodmancote, Woolstone and Oxenton.[39]

Other resources were put under pressure. On the top of Nottingham Hill lay the common waste, important for pasturing animals. In order to prevent overcommoning here and on the fallow fields, attempts were made to limit the number of animals the tenants could own, depending upon the size of their holding. Despite the attempts at regulation, this was often haphazard in practice. In 1555 one holding of fifty-two acres held rights of common for sixty animals; another holding of twenty-eight acres held rights for fifty-two.[40] Coppice wood for hurdles and furniture came from Gotherington Grove which was larger than it is today, and from an area behind Moat Farm. Some of the trees may have been left to grow for timber

54

which would also have come from individual trees growing around the settlements. On Nottingham Hill lay the quarries, necessary for building material. The lord owned the rights and granted licences for the extraction of the stone. There is just one reference, in the court rolls for 1414, to the men of Gotherington taking stone without licence.[41] Perhaps this was the one occasion when the bishop actually took action against a long-established practice.

As we read in Chapter 1, the main watercourse for both communities flowed down from Nottingham Hill above the manor-house. Keeping the water clean and free-running as it made its various ways down through the village was of concern to all the community. In 1414 the abbot was fined by the bishops for not cleaning the ditch at 'le Dyke';[42] in 1504 there was a general order against washing clothes or throwing animal garbage into the brook or diverting the water.[43] For most of its route the watercourse can now no longer be traced on the ground surface.

The post-war development of Gotherington has destroyed much of the late medieval settlement and trackway pattern. The map shows only those areas which can be reconstructed with reasonable certainty. The planned settlement for the ex-slaves can be identified below the manor-house. The main area of the settlement lies further west, around the present village centre, where the holdings of tenants of Upper and Lower Gotherington met. The area extends westwards to include the freehold farms at Lower Gotherington. Some existing houses in these areas are likely to date back to the very end of the Middle Ages.

By the early sixteenth century this medieval landscape was changing: arable strips were being put down to permanent pasture and enclosed by hedges on the lower slopes of Nottingham Hill, and the nucleated area around the manor house was in full decline with decaying houses and abandoned plots.[44] But change was not confined to the landscape. The religious upheavals of the reign of Henry VIII led to the removal of the church as the landlord of the villagers of Gotherington. The land of the bishop's manor seems to have gone to the freehold tenants; the land of the abbot's manor went to Richard Weller, the abbot's tenant. The records which he and later owners kept allow us to trace Gotherington's history nearer to our own day. This forms the subject of Chapter 6.

Cotswold Cottage is another house in Shutter Lane which dates back to the end of the Middle Ages. In 1843 it was the home of Hannah Harris whose possessions are described in Chapter 7

References

1   J.H. Round, *Studies in Peerage and Family History* (Westminster, 1901), p. 190.
2   *Book of Fees*, Part I (London, 1920), p. 39.
3   *Dictionary of National Biography*, Vol. V (London, 1886), p. 25.
4   S.B. Burke, *A Genealogical History of the Dormant, Abeyance, Forfeited and Extinct Peerages* (London, 1866), p. 53; W. Dugdale, *Monasticon Anglicanum*, Vol. II (London, 1849), p. 78.
5   J. Bennett, *The History of Tewkesbury* (Tewkesbury, 1830), p. 102.
6   D.M. Stenton (ed.), *Rolls of the Justices in Eyre for Gloucestershire, Warwickshire and Staffordshire, 1221, 1222* (Seldon Society, Vol. 59, 1940), p. 112.
7   *Valor Ecclesiasticus*, Vol. II (London, 1814), p. 478.
8   Gloucestershire Record Office (GRO) D184 M19.
9   S.J. Madge and E.A. Fry (ed.), *Inquisitiones Post Mortem for Gloucestershire*, Vol. V (British Record Society, 1910), pp. 118–19.
10 M. Hollings (ed.), *Red Book of Worcester* (RBW), Vol. IV (Worcester Historical Society (WHS), 1950), pp. 350–3. A second survey was taken in 1299 and is printed on pp. 327–47 in the same volume.
11 Ibid., pp. 350–3.
12 Ibid., pp. 327–47.
13 A grant of land in Lower Gotherington *c.* 1260 was witnessed, *inter alia*, by Richard and Henry Bigod and Simon Pendock; D. Royce (ed.), *Landboc sive Registrum Monasterii . . . de Wincelumba*, Vol. I (Exeter, 1892), pp. 114–16. The editor adds a note that he has lately discovered a seal of green wax of Simon Pendock – another indication he was acting like a lord of the manor in Gotherington.
14 The bulk of the manorial records for Bishop's Cleeve are in the Worcestershire Record Office (WRO) under the reference 009:1BA 2636. The references given in this chapter to these records will be to the parcel number and individual record number, viz for this reference WRO: 193/92628 9/9.
15 WRO: 161/92113 4/6.
16 1540 survey: GRO: P329 M15; 1555 survey: GRO: D184 M19.
17 *Gloucestershire Subsidy Roll*, I Edward III, 1327 (Middlehill Press, n.d.), p. 28.
18 GRO: D184 M12.
19 GRO: D184 M19.
20 *c.* 1170 and 1299: see ref. 10 above; *c.* 1475: WRO: 161/921113 3/6; 1327: see ref. 17 above.
21 J.W. Willis Bund (ed.), *Register of Bishop Godfrey Giffard* (WHS 1898–1902), p. 306.
22 WRO: 162/92117.
23 C.C. Dyer, *Standards of Living in the Later Middle Ages* (Cambridge, 1989), pp. 110–18.
24 GRO: D184/M9.
25 GRO: D184/T59.
26 GRO: D184/M9.
27 GRO: P329 M15.
28 WRO: 192/92627 2/12.
29 References starting with Walter are as follows: Willis Bund, *Giffard* p. 306; J.W. Willis Bund and R.A. Wilson (eds), *Register of William of Geynesburgh, Bishop of Worcester 1302–7* (WHS, 1907 and 1929), p. 137; E.H. Pearce (ed.), *Register of Thomas Cobham 1317–27* (WHS, 1930), p. 22; R.M. Haines (ed.), *A Calendar of the Register of Adam of Orleton 1327–33* (London, 1979), p. 13; J. Willis Bund (ed.), *Registrum Sede Vacante* (WHS, 1897), p. 35; W.P. Marrett (ed.), *A Calendar of the Register of Henry Wakefield* (WHS, 1972), pp. 65, 221.

30 H.R. Luard (ed.), *Annales Monastici*, Vol. I (London, 1864), p. 86.

31 *Hockaday Abstracts*, Vol. 129 in Gloucester Library, quoting Register of Archbishop Islep, folio 146a in Lambeth Palace, London. A priest was recorded at Gotherington in the 1327 Lay Subsidy.

32 WRO: 162/92115.

33 WRO: 174/92170 6/6; 162/92117.

34 WRO: 174/92470 6/6.

35 WRO: 162/92115; 193/92628 9/9.

36 WRO: 162/92115.

37 WRO: 192/92627 2/12.

38 The aerial photographs of Gotherington were consulted at the Royal Commission for Historical Monuments, Fleming Way, Swindon, Wilts.

39 See C.C. Dyer, *Standards of Living in the Later Middle Ages* (Cambridge, 1989), p. 111 for a similar map of the manor of Bishop's Cleeve.

40 GRO: D184 M19.

41 WRO: 193/92628 9/19.

42 Ibid.

43 WRO: 162/92122.

44 GRO: P329 M15.

CHAPTER SIX

The Manor in the Hands of the Gentry

Gotherington in the Period 1550–1808

Geoffrey Pitt and Eunice Powell

This period opens at a time when the whole country was having to adjust to rapid changes of ecclesiastical policy and was suffering severe inflation which only gradually stabilized in the reign of Elizabeth. It ends with the enclosure of the open fields – the most important event in Gotherington's history. By 1550 the dissolution of the monastic institutions had brought very large land holdings into the king's hand, many of which were sold to replenish the royal coffers, thus transferring much of the economic power previously wielded by the Church to secular lords of the manor. By the early years of the seventeenth century, the returning prosperity left London merchants with profits to invest in run-down rural estates for the regular income they provided, but not apparently with any intention of carrying out improvements.

THE DEVELOPMENT OF THE CRAVEN ESTATE

In this area of Gloucestershire, many communities were adversely affected by the dissolution of the abbeys at Tewkesbury, Winchcombe and Hailes and the priory at Deerhurst which had provided markets for their produce.[1] From the Tewkesbury Abbey estates the manors of Upper Gotherington, Pamington, Tredington and Great Washbourne were held by the crown from 1539 to 1557 when the Catholic Queen Mary granted them to the widow of Sir Adrian Fortescue in recognition of his refusal to acknowledge Henry VIII as head of the church, for which he had been beheaded in 1539. The Fortescues were already an established family in the lesser nobility, one Sir John Fortescue having been Lord Chief Justice in Henry VI's reign and another was to become Chancellor of the Exchequer to Queen Elizabeth in 1589. They do not appear to have prized the local manors highly for they sold them sixty-four years later to the widow of Sir William Craven, a very successful self-made man, a member of the Merchant Taylors company and Lord Mayor of London.[2] The purchase price for Gotherington manor was £2,392, which was twenty times the annual income from rents, so a return of 5 per cent was assured.[3]

The Cravens acquired numerous estates including a total of six thousand acres in Gloucestershire and many more in sixteen other counties of England and Wales. Their houses were in London and Berkshire and from there they exercised businesslike control through stewards who collected the rents and presided at the annual meeting (court baron) which all tenants were required to attend. Sir William Craven's son became successively a baron, viscount and earl, devoting much of his very long life and considerable fortune to the Stuart cause. As a consequence his estates were forfeited during the Commonwealth and sold for the benefit of the navy. The manor of Gotherington was purchased by Philip Starkey, a luckless cook in the City who must have seen his investment vanish seven years later when Lord Craven regained his estates at the restoration in 1660. Thereafter the manor remained under Craven control until 1853.[4]

The manor lands amounted to about one thousand acres and they were divided into parcels which as far as can be established remained the same from before 1550 to at least 1724. The Craven estate, therefore, kept largely intact the medieval manor of Upper Gotherington which had been held by Tewkesbury Abbey. Much the largest holding was the manor farm, of about three hundred acres, which was also unique in having over 40 per cent of its land in 'closes', that is in enclosed fields as we know them as opposed to strips in open fields. As explained in Chapter 5, these lay around the manor-house itself. The remaining twenty holdings ranged from about fifty acres to one and a half acres, with the great majority of their land in the open fields, although most had one or more small closes adjoining the homestead.[5]

By the mid-sixteenth century the classical pattern of agriculture in the Severn vale based on two open fields had changed into a three field rotation system in which corn crops were grown for two years, followed by a fallow year to restore the fertility. The system of fields in Gotherington seems, however, to have been more complex than the text-book three field pattern. There are many references to strips (or lands or selions) in named fields in documents from this period but some inconsistencies and at no stage were there just three fields. The following names have been identified from the surveys:

1552	1630	1724	1775	1808
Denne	Deane	Dean	Dean	Dean
Glee Hill	Clayhill	Clay	Clayhill	Clayhill
Salis	Sally	Sally	Sallow	
Myddle	Grastons	Grasston	Grasston	
Hichin			Cowlesworth	
Over			Upper	

There are also many named furlongs in these documents (a furlong normally being a group of parallel strips lying together in a field). The location of a tenant's strips is frequently specified as being in a certain furlong without any mention of the field, which may perhaps suggest that these furlongs were separately cultivated from the rest of the field from before 1550. Some field and furlong names are shown on the map overleaf.[6]

The court rolls give many examples of the way in which the manor was managed, though they never specify which crops were to be grown in which fields during the coming year. The tenants at the annual court baron would present matters for the attention of the presiding steward:

1556 Homage (the assembled tenants) present Richard Taylor . . . for keeping subtenants against the order – penalty incurred 40s.

18 October 1667 . . . presents Thomas Rogers as a common hedge breaker – in mercy (i.e. fined) 6s 8d. If not paid by 1 November Thomas Rogers to be beaten in the stocks. (His annual rent was only 1s 9d.)

1689 . . . present that Jonathan Ensigne keeps a disorderly alehouse . . .

1692 . . . present the death of Joan Barradell. Homage recommend to the lord to grant her tenement to John Leech her kinsman. (Later in the meeting John Leech of

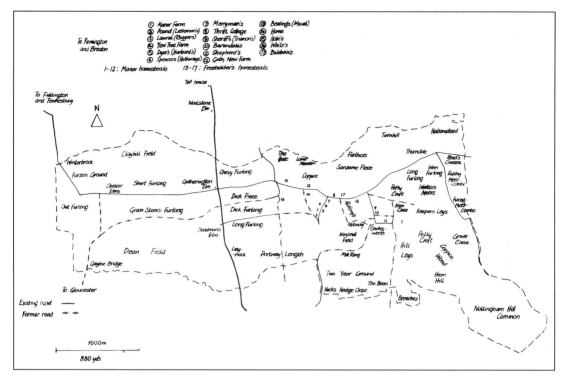

A composite map of the parish showing the position of the farms and many of the features mentioned in this and the preceding chapters

Gotherington, collar-marker, was admitted to the one tenement and quarter yardland for the lives of John Leech, Mary his wife and John his son at a yearly rent of 8s 6d. The tenancy would therefore last as long as at least one of the three people named survived, up to a maximum of ninety-nine years.)

These and other similar orders suggest that the ups and downs of manorial life had changed little since the later Middle Ages.

Orders were frequently made concerning such matters as having all pigs ringed, not letting more than the permitted number of animals on the common, keeping the ditches scoured, providing stone for the repair of the pound where stray animals were kept, and making boundary mounds around the cornfields to keep animals out. Subcommittees of jurors were often deputed to settle boundary disputes: '. . . on petition of William Aston, jurors to meet at 10 o'clock next Monday to view land between Dick Furlong and Chiver Furlong and fix boundaries, putting doleholes between as these ought to be. To report to the next court – penalty (for non-compliance) 5s'. It is of interest to note that these two furlongs lie on either side of the present Malleson Road where it approaches the Evesham Road, so the occurrence of a boundary dispute in 1696 suggests that there was no road there then.[7] The court rolls were written for the benefit of the lord's steward as he and his clerk would probably be the only persons present able to read, and certainly the only ones able to understand the Latin in which they were written. There were no 'copies of the minutes of the meeting' circulated!

Since such meetings were held only once a year, the degree of control exercised by the Cravens could not have been as great as that of lords of the manor who lived in their villages. The villagers of Gotherington were well-used to absentee landlords. Gotherington developed into a typical 'open' village in contrast to 'closed' villages like Whittington where the manor-house, parish church and rectory overlooked the village and the lord of the manor and the rector could dictate the running of the community every day. Open villages were more likely to gain 'squatters' who would build a small cottage on waste land or on the roadside without permission, although they would probably have to face the lord's steward later. In 1667, Anthony Webb the elder, labourer, had to pay an entry fine of £5 for the lease of 'the little piece of ground now in his possession [1 rood] on which he erected a cottage; lying upon the Mill Way and adjacent to Alcrofte: yearly rent 12d'.[8] Open villages tended to develop in an untidy straggling fashion as a result of such enterprise and they were more likely to acquire tradesmen and Nonconformists. Several of the older houses in the village were built during this period and in this way.

As indicated above, there was very little, if any, change in the land holdings from before 1550 to at least 1724. Individual holdings can be traced from one survey or lease to another by the unchanging and peculiarly precise annual rents (£1 16s 4½d, 5s and four capons, . . .) and by much of the description of the land held. One of the best examples of how the land units remained essentially unchanged for a very long time is provided by Truman's Farm in Manor Lane. The holding appears in a number of surveys as follows:

1540/1552   John Sheriff by copy 1 messuage, 3 small closes, 1½ acres in Deane field, 1 acre Clee Hill, ½ acre Winterbroke, 1 sellion Chevye furlong, 1 acre Dyche, 1½ acre Long furlong, 1 sellion Lammas Heye, 1 sellion Haustowe, ½ acre and 1 farndel above Haustowe, 1 acre Breches, 2 acres Over. Rent 15s.

1630   Frances Shrefe, widow 60, holds 1 messuage and appurtenances, 1 close of pasture, The Croft, half of close of pasture The Paddock, 1 acre in Dean, 1 acre Clayell, ½ acre shuting in Wynter Brooke, 1 ridge Chever furlong, 2 acres Ditch, 1½ acres Long Furlong, ½ acre shuting on Haustway, 1 acre Breaches, Total 13 acres, 3 rods, 24 perches. Rent 15s.

1724   William Shrief, 70, holds for his life a dwelling house of 3 bays, a barn of 3 bays, stable, garden, yard and a little close adjoining, close of meadow

Manor Farm · Truemans

Truman's Farm in Manor Lane is now the last remaining working farm that links back to the Middle Ages

61

The Croft, half a close called The Paddock, close of pasture Short Close, and arable in Dean (¾ acre), Clay furlong (¾ acre), Short furlong and Winterbrook (¾ acre), Cheever (½ acre), Ditch (1¼ acres), Long furlong (1¼ acres), Hostway (¼ acre), Breach (½ acre). Rent 15s.

1768   Kinard Sheriff (deceased) held a house, yard and garden, the Croft, Short Close, Dean (½ acre), Clay Hill (½ acre), Short furlong, Winterbrook, Chevy (1 acre), Ditch (1 acre), Long furlong (2 acres), The Breach (1 acre).

1808   Kinner's house and adjoining orchard are listed among the Craven tofts and closes [Kinner = Kinard, see above].

1839   James Hobbs was tenant of Kinner's house, orchard and a total of 54 acres.

1894   House is called Truman's Farm, land is reduced to about 15 acres by rearrangement.

By present day standards it seems incredible that rents remained the same over a period approaching two centuries, especially when a survey carried out in 1630, nine years after the Cravens purchased the manor, indicated that the total income from rents ought to be nearly three times as great as it was.[9] The surveyor commented, for example, that 'there belongeth to this manor very large and good commons on the Top of the Hill called by the name of Nottingham and the tenants may put in these for every yardland, forty sheep or more and the scope which they have to feed in is three or four hundred acres at the least which if the same be well employed may be made very beneficial both to the Farme and the rest of the Tenants'. Here is a more precise statement on 'stinting' than could be found for the later Middle Ages. It indicates how commercial farming was demanding enclosed private fields on land which was part of the community's assets, a process which was to culminate in the Act of Inclosure of 1808. The same surveyor pointed out:

There is a Coppice Wood lying on the side of the Hill above the Farm [which] containeth by estimation 12 acres rated one year with another at £4. Which if the same were layd so that there might every year be one acre felled at twelve years growth then the same would be sold for £5 the acre at least.

Total (present) rental of the whole Manor	£124 19s ½d
Improvement	£220

It does not seem that any action was taken on the suggested ways to increase the income from the manor, possibly because Lord Craven owned many manors, never married and had no dependants to provide for.

AGRICULTURAL IMPROVEMENT

There is no evidence that the Cravens did anything to change the pattern of farming here until the eighteenth century. Although the manor rents remained unchanged until then, there was one particular progressive change which would have increased the average annual income from the manor. When a new lease was awarded, the incoming tenant had to pay an entry fine for the privilege which, though not in strict proportion to the rent, was roughly equal to one year's rent between 1530 and 1550 when leases were granted for one lifetime. A century later, when leases were granted for two or three lives and were therefore more valuable, entry fines had increased disproportionately to the equivalent of about twenty years' rent, and by 1700 they had reached about sixty years' rent. In practice leases for three lives lasted for between five and fifty years so the increasing entry fines represented a significant rise in the effective rent averaged over the duration of the lease, particularly when the lease ended in a very short time.

In addition there must have been potential tenants unable to find the larger sums demanded. Information on leases after 1728 is lacking, but in that year one lease was granted with a rent of £1 and an entry fine of £308. Moreover the tenant was to be charged £10 for each acre of old meadow or pasture ploughed up, an indication of the potential profit to be gained then by switching from pasture to arable crops.[10]

The steep increase in entry fines may have been a move to make up the loss of income during the forfeiture in the 1650s and later to recoup the land tax introduced at the end of the seventeenth century to pay for the 'Marlborough' wars on the Continent. It is unlikely that there was any marked improvement in the profitability of farming locally over this period to justify higher effective rents, even though pioneering agricultural writers were advocating changes in methods of farming such as the proper rotation of crops, land drainage and the growing of turnips, potatoes and clover. These would in time lead to increased arable yields and better fed livestock, but such changes were difficult in the open field system. The advantages to be gained by their introduction provided a strong argument for supporters of enclosure. If the open field lands were redistributed to give individual farmers a number of fields, each surrounded by a hedge and ditch, it would become worthwhile for them to invest in the installation of land drains and there would be greater freedom of choice of the crops to be grown. The farmer could also improve his stock by selective breeding and by reducing the risk of infection, spread when the community's animals were put out to graze as one herd on the fallow field under the care of a hayward.

Some small enclosed fields had existed since the later Middle Ages around Manor Farm for which the tenant paid a very high rent, and it appears that a little more may have been achieved in the 1760s when the Cravens bought out some small local landowners, and carried out some measure of rearrangement of the holdings. Seven of the Craven smallholdings (all under ten acres) were added to the melting pot from which three new larger farms appeared, each of about one hundred and fifty acres, with between twenty and forty acres each in enclosed land. These were Gotherington New Farm (later Brick House Farm, now The

Brick House Farm

Pullen Court was built on the site of the yard, barn and pond of Yew Tree Farm, seen here before demolition by 1970. The farmhouse still survives

Dower House), Bealing's Farm (previously the freehold farm held in Lower Gotherington by the Pendock family and not part of the Craven's first purchase, now Moat Farm), and a third which was unnamed in 1768, later Yew Tree Farm.[11] Clearly they were modern farms with large well-constructed farmhouses for which high rents could be charged. They are important in Gotherington's history for they make the first clear change to a pattern of farming which had remained largely unchanged from the fifteenth century. They mark the arrival of a clearly commercial approach to agriculture, and the destruction of medieval faming units in Upper Gotherington. In fact, by 1801 the rents of these three farms plus Manor Farm totalled £636 whereas all the rest of the rents added up to less than £50 and one tenant was still paying the time-honoured £1 1s 7½d for an unimproved farm of twenty-five acres.[12] One of the attractions of the large farms was undoubtedly the availability of some enclosed land but this was limited and the argument for enclosure of the common fields must have grown more forceful year by year among the better-off farmers.

In many parts of the country the enclosure movement developed rapidly during the eighteenth century and became highly organized with the passage of private acts of parliament to override local opposition, by which parliamentary commissioners were appointed to re-allocate the land in the open fields and commons. The act for Gotherington was passed in 1806.[13] Under its terms the modern fieldscape of Gotherington was created and the ridge and furrow was criss-crossed by new, straight hedges and ditches. The act empowered the commissioner to allot land to the rector of Bishop's Cleeve in lieu of tithes, so Gotherington became tithe-free, at a price. The rector's allotment was to be equivalent in value to one fifth of the arable land and one ninth of the meadow and pasture, and it was clearly stated in the act that burial fees, Easter offerings and surplice fees were not abolished. Tithes had always been a source of great grievance among farmers who saw no reason why the rector should have a tenth of all their produce – sometimes selected by the rector in person! The fractions of land

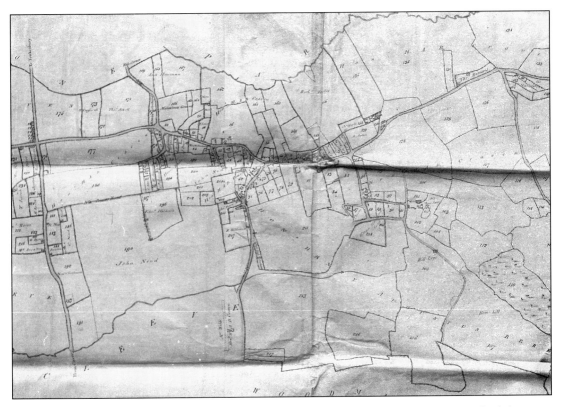

Part of the enclosure map showing the centre of Gotherington. In 1807 there were still buildings in the plots below Manor Farm (GRO: Q/RI71 by permission)

to be given up at enclosure were higher than one tenth because it was argued that the rector would now be getting the wherewithal to produce crops rather than the crops themselves and he would have to pay for the farm labour required. It would have been interesting to hear the comments at that time in the Gotherington Inn (which later became the Shutter Inn) concerning the rector having fifths and ninths of the land!

The act also made provision for parcels of land to be sold by auction to defray the expenses of enclosure, roughly 7 per cent being marked out for this purpose. Included in these expenses was the cost of making boundary fences to the rector's tithe allotment and keeping them in repair for seven years, to be recovered from the other landowners. After the passing of the act events moved swiftly. The commissioner appointed in June 1806 was John Stone who came from Pull Court near Tewkesbury and had acted in other enclosures; he had a surveyor, Samuel Harris, from Gloucester to assist him. Their task required a complete survey of the 1,643 acres involved, holding meetings to establish claims to land and grazing rights and making some assessment of the relative values of different areas of land. Then a map had to be prepared on a large enough scale (12 inches to the mile) to define new boundaries and act as a reference in the event of disputes. One man appealed against the boundary but lost his case, and by January 1808 the commissioner was able to complete his work with the preparation of the statutory duplicate copies (on numerous large pieces of parchment) of the Enclosure Award, one copy of which can now be inspected in the Gloucestershire Record Office.[14] It comprises the map, a document called a terrier which defines all the two hundred and fifty plots of land, a detailed list of all the allotments, their new owners and the responsibility for the boundary fences.

The land was allocated generally according to the amount of land held before the enclosure. The largest allocations were inevitably to the lord of the manor, the Hon. Henry Augustus Berkeley Craven, with nearly half the total area, and the rector of Bishop's Cleeve who gained a large part of the land to the south of Gotherington Fields Road down to the Dean Brook (about one sixth of the total area). Five freeholders were allotted between ten and a hundred acres each, while about thirty others obtained smaller allocations. Finally there were twenty allocations to those who lost their grazing rights on the commonland, principally as a result of the enclosure of Nottingham Hill Common. These were concentrated in two areas, one at the north-west corner of the crossroads on the Evesham Road, the other behind Gorse Green Cottage on the Gretton Road. Most of them were less than ten perches and six were two perches (50 sq m) or roughly one-quarter of the size of a singles tennis court. The set by the Evesham Road would have been liable to pilfering from passers-by, being remote from all housing at that time; clearly a quite inadequate exchange for the right to keep a pig or a goose on Nottingham Hill. There is no evidence that these tiny plots were ever worked and it seems possible that they were subsequently exchanged for land elsewhere. According to the deeds of Jasmine Cottage in Shutter Lane it was built on land 'acquired by Samuel Reeves in exchange for pasturage rights at the time of the Enclosure Award'; the award shows that he was allotted ten perches behind Gorse Green Cottage.[15] No time was to be wasted in bringing about the changes. Ten weeks were allowed from the date of the award in mid-January in which new owners of fields were required to complete their enclosure: 'fences to be made with posts and three rails on each side with stays between posts, the rails to be nailed to the posts with pairs of ten penny nails, and quick set hedges and 3ft wide ditches 2ft deep'. This was hard work over and above the normal tasks on the farm, but obviously necessary in order that the spring sowing should not be missed.

ATTEMPTS TO IMPROVE THE ROADS

The award also listed five new public roads and six private roads which were to be constructed to specified widths between hedges. It is difficult to be sure what was meant by 'new' roads in this context because the only know pre-enclosure local map does not mark roads unless they adjoin the enclosed manor fields.[16] Some may have been entirely new but it seems probable that most were upgraded from those already in use. Three of the public roads were to be a standard 30 ft wide:

1   From the corner of Woolstone Lane in Malleson Road westwards to Gotherington Fields and then north towards the junction near Bozard's Farm.
2   Turning south from 1 beyond Gotherington Fields Farm to Guyloe Bridge over the Dean Brook, described as the Gloucester Road. It was already in existence before enclosure with a quite sizeable bridge, the remains of which can still be seen today although the road is now no more than a footpath. From Guyloe Bridge the line of the old road can be discerned on an Ordnance Survey map, following the south-east side of the Stoke Orchard airfield to Elmstone Hardwicke, Withy Bridge and Staverton. It is of interest to note that there is a footpath continuing the line of Shutter Lane westwards across the Evesham Road below the White House and along field boundaries to Guyloe Bridge. This may have been the old road out of Gotherington to pick up either the road from Bredon and Pamington to Gloucester or one through Fiddington and Walton Cardiff to Tewkesbury from the junction near Bozard's farm.
3   From the top of Granna Lane across Nottingham Hill.

This footpath in Gotherington Fields was the road to Gloucester in 1806 and probably for many centuries before that

The other two public roads were to be 25 ft wide between hedges:

4   The Cleeve Road from the last house in Gotherington 'passing into the parish of
     Bishops Cleeve'.
5   The short stretch of Woolstone Lane between the last house in Gotherington and the
     pair of farm cottages just in Woolstone parish.

No explanation can be offered why Cleeve Road should be only 25 ft wide when it must
have carried a good deal of traffic then as now. The private roads were 15 ft or less in width
and provided access to otherwise isolated plots of land, most of them now being no more than
farm tracks.

    The only road out of the village not scheduled for improvement in the award was the one
to Gretton, presumably because it was considered already adequate for the traffic using it. This
very old road from the ancient town of Winchcombe leading eventually to the Severn at
Deerhurst had long since lost much of its importance with the decline of Winchcombe. Some
roads in the village also lost their importance after the eighteenth century as shown on the
map on page 60. They became paths or vanished altogether.

    The roads in the Severn vale were notoriously bad in the eighteenth century, made worse
by the increasing volume of traffic. William Marshall described them in 1796 as often mere
quagmires with ditches on either side full of water.[17] The Cheltenham to Gloucester road was
likened to the bed of a river in the rainy season and there were tales of horses sinking to their
death in the mud. Much of the trade of the vale was with Bristol and went by the Severn, but
the farm produce had first to be transported from the surrounding villages to Tewkesbury,
whether for shipment or for sale in the market or for milling.

    The coming of a network of turnpike roads radiating from Tewkesbury from 1726 onwards
should have eased the problems but initially the roads were not properly maintained, and even

as late as the last quarter of the eighteenth century farmers from Bishop's Cleeve and Gotherington had to take corn to Tewkesbury on the backs of horses because the roads were impassable for wagons or carts.[18] It was only at the beginning of the nineteenth century that matters improved after Road Clubs were formed to put pressure on the trustees of the turnpikes.

It is difficult to establish the details of the road system in this area as it seems to have undergone many changes. Numerous acts of parliament gave turnpike trustees the power to maintain and improve roads by exacting tolls from travellers but information on the implementation of the acts is almost non-existent. Many of the schemes proposed were never put into action or were superseded by new proposals. The turnpike road from Bishop's Cleeve to Tewkesbury via Aston Cross was proposed in 1755 and was certainly in operation for seventy years from 1802 onwards, the right to collect tolls at the Pike House on the Evesham Road being auctioned annually during this period.[19] The growing importance of Cheltenham at the end of the eighteenth century led to the old road from Bishop's Cleeve via Kayte Lane, Southam and Prestbury being replaced by a completely new direct road (the A435 before the construction of the Bishop's Cleeve bypass) in 1810. Other turnpike acts included one for the Winchcombe–Gretton–Gotherington–Bishop's Cleeve road and, almost unbelievably, for the prehistoric trackway from Gotherington up Crannel (Granna) Lane to the top of Gotherington Hill (1755), extended in 1794 across Cleeve Cloud to the Syreford Inn near Whittington, and still included in later acts up to 1826, although it never did become a turnpike road.[20]

THE HOMES OF THE VILLAGERS

The Craven documents relating to the manor have been carefully preserved but inevitably they tell us very little about the twenty or so copyhold tenants at any given time, even less about the three or four freeholders and nothing about the rest of the inhabitants. Reliable figures for the population only become available in the nineteenth century, although approximate estimates can be made at a number of earlier dates which indicate about 200 to 250 people up to the early eighteenth century increasing to 335 by 1801, not many less than in Bishop's Cleeve. Only by this later date had the figures reached the totals suggested for the two Gotheringtons in 1299 in Chapter 5.

One of the few sources of contemporary evidence on the daily lives and possessions of the ordinary villagers, the freehold and tenant farmers, is to be found in the probate inventories of the period but even then it is rare to find the poorer members of the community represented. From Elizabethan times to 1859 probate of a will required that a detailed inventory be made of a deceased person's 'goods, chattels and cattle' by two appraisors (persons of some standing in the community, perhaps churchwardens).

About twenty inventories of Gotherington people of the seventeenth and eighteenth centuries have survived the rigours of being 'placed in a dirty hole in one end of Bishop's Cleeve church where, by great dint of chance, the Deputy Registrar found them about the year 1819 soddened with wet and so much mutilated as to render many unintelligible.'[21] As would be expected in Gotherington all the deceased in this sample had carried on some form of agriculture, mainly arable, but with some livestock. As a rule the appraisors listed and valued crops and animals with more accuracy than household goods which were often lumped together as 'all iron things', 'brass and pewter' and 'other lumber'. In reading inventories it must be remembered that the possessions were usually those of someone late in life who had probably settled much of his or her property on the children beforehand and so it should not seem too remarkable that, for instance, Thomas Holland 'gentleman' of Moat Farm had no more than £23 in goods at his death in 1690/1, including two chairs, a little table board, a flagon, two pewter dishes, a candlestick, a brass pan and pot, a chest and a trunk, a bed, two blankets and two pairs of sheets in addition to some farming goods; the only items indicative of a higher standard of living were two table-cloths, half a dozen napkins and a tun of coal.[22]

In contrast Daniel Finch's inventory (1728) is clearly that of a flourishing farmer who had been still in business with possessions valued at £471. He had commitments for rent as a manor tenant of forty acres and also had an outstanding bond and mortgage on other land which he was using to increase his acreage of wheat to seventy. The appraisers cast a practised eye over the farm animals and valued separately the cows, heifers, yearlings, calves, bull, colts, mares, gelding, sheep, pigs and roasting pigs but took less time over the household items ending (with relief) 'for lumber and things not mentioned'. In fact, linen and bedding were valued at £15, furniture at less than £3 and household implements £6.[23]

Alice Aston, a widow who actively continued her husband's leasehold tenancy, had possessions valued at £265 in 1725/6 including 114 sheep and crops of wheat, barley, pulses and hay; her only apparent luxury item was a clock.[24] William Ward was also the owner of a clock in 1761 together with a 'beaurdaw' (an item of furniture which caused the appraisers some difficulty). The Wards carried on their occupation of maltsters for at least three generations at the Malt Shovel in Shutter Lane, and William's 'old stock of malt' was worth £9 in a total of £151, most of which arose from farming stock and equipment.[25] These last three inventories are much above the average in value, other examples noted ranging from £12 to £43, including those of three larger farmers.

The average dwelling in the village at this time was a four-roomed cottage, as for example, Woodbine Cottage in Gretton Road. They were clearly very sparsely furnished, in keeping with J.S. Moore's finding that 'it was comparatively rare for furniture and domestic equipment in the seventeenth and early eighteenth centuries to exceed £30 in value and it quite commonly totalled £10 to £25'.[26] With a basic diet of bread and beer, and a rented cottage in a bad (or very bad) state of repair, the typical villager had a spartan existence, but clearly above the level of his/her medieval counterpart. As far as we know, peasants no longer starved.

THE VILLAGERS

There are also occasional opportunities to gain other impressions of the village people from the archives. In 1608, for example, fears of a Spanish invasion recurred and a survey of all potential defenders was carried out in Gloucestershire.[27] Fifty-three Gotherington men were listed by name, rank or trade, in three age groups from twenty to sixty approximately, and in categories of physique: would they be best suited to wield a pike, carry a musket or be a pioneer? Limited and incomplete as this is, it is of great interest coming more than two hundred years before the first detailed national census. It lists three gentlemen (who would not expect to work with their hands), one of whom, Nicholas Weller, lived at Manor Farm and the other two, William and Thomas Holland (father and son) probably both lived at Moat Farm. Then came six 'yeomen' (five of them in one family) and ten 'husbandmen', both terms for men who worked land as freeholders or tenants. There were ten craftsmen (four carpenters, three tailors, a smith, a weaver and a glover), twelve labourers and twelve men for whom no occupation was given – perhaps they were paupers or servants in the better-off households. Only four of the fifty-three were in the oldest age group (about fifty to sixty years old), no doubt due in part to the lower life expectancy in those days but also to a high proportion of men of that age being deemed unfit for military service. As might be expected, physique was on average somewhat better in the upper classes and poorer in those with no stated occupation. Six of the better-off men were prepared to pay a subsidy man to fight in their place, and one labourer was a trained soldier.

This view of a community still totally dependent upon agricultural related trades is supplemented two generations later by a list of those liable to pay the Hearth Tax in 1671–2 as

January 22
1728

A true and perfect Inventory of all the Goods
Cattle & Chattle that Daniel Finch of Gotheringtton
In the parish of Bishops Cleeve in the County
of Gloucester Dyed possessed off

	£	S	D
Money in purse & Wearing Apparell	11	00	00
5 Cows valued att	10	00	00
69 Acers of Corn & a half valued	127	12	06
4 Hifers valued at	14	00	00
5 Earling valued at	12	10	00
2 Colts and a Bull valued at	12	00	00
3 Calves & a Colt valued	05	10	00
5 Mares and a Gelding valued at	29	04	00
47 Sheep valued at	18	10	00
6 Piggs valued at	02	02	00
For Rosting Piggs valued at	00	12	00
For a Small Stack of Hay valued	01	10	00
For Hay in the Craft valued	04	00	00
For Ricks of Hay in ye Backside	10	00	00
For Hay	03	10	00
3 Fans a bushell & a Sive	00	13	06
4 ploughs 2 pair of Harrows & 2 Drags	02	10	00
2 Wagons & a Dung Cart	17	00	00
5 piggs valued att	03	01	00
For Horse Harnish & Paniels	05	00	00
For Beding in ye Room over ye Kitching	04	17	08
For a Chest and Coffers	00	16	00
For Beding in ye Hall Chamber	04	19	02
For Blanketts	00	15	00
2 Bedsteds	00	08	00
For Coffers a Chest & a box	00	18	00
For Blanketts a bolster a ty & a pair of bed	00	14	00
For 2 Bedsteds	00	09	00
	297	12	10

A typical probate inventory of 1728. Daniel Finch was a wealthy man, but most of his wealth was tied up in his farm, especially in his corn crop (By kind permission of the Right Reverend the Bishop of Gloucester: GDR: Bishop's Cleeve Will No. 18)

Woodbine Cottage dates possibly from the seventeenth century, but it was a typical home for a labourer in the eighteenth and nineteenth centuries. Its exterior remains largely unaltered. The chapel was built in 1833

occupiers of premises with one or more hearths.[28] Thirty-one people were required to pay and thirty were considered too poor to do so. Mr Cross at Manor Farm had eight hearths, two other gentlemen – one living at Moat House – had six and three to pay for, and of the others, three had three hearths, twelve had two and thirteen had one. All except one of those discharged from paying had only one hearth as would be expected in small cottages. It appears that there was a high level of poverty but it is not known to what extent the collector had discretion to relieve the poor from paying.

THE POOR

From the earliest days the duty of relieving the poor, legally the responsibility of the manor, was generally accepted as morally falling upon the church. Vagrants and beggars presented a growing problem, especially during the upheavals of Henry VIII's reign, and legislation was introduced to force individual parishes to care for their own poor, culminating in the 1601 Poor Law Act which made churchwardens responsible for taxing the inhabitants to generate the wherewithal to maintain the poor. Gotherington was part of the larger Bishop's Cleeve parish for purposes of civil and ecclesiastical administration and thus came under the authority of the vestry. This was a select body of some two dozen of the principal inhabitants of the parish, largely self-recruiting, under the chairmanship of the rector within whose control lay the appointment of unpaid officers – churchwardens, overseers of the poor, waywardens and constables; it was a forerunner of the parish council.

These appointed officers kept records and accounts which were submitted annually to the vestry after having been officially agreed by the local justices of the peace. It is from the vestry minutes and the accounts of the officers, particularly the overseer of the poor, that one can trace parish life at the level of the ordinary worker and the poor.[29] The vestry fixed a poor rate

71

to be levied from householders and had the right to determine who should pay and who should be excused. The amount disbursed among the poor in Gotherington rose from £40 in 1750 to about £200 in 1800. There were low years and peak years but it is impossible to say with any certainty what caused these. So many factors were involved such as the incidence of disease and unemployment, poor wages, poor harvest, the price of bread, the impact of the French Wars after 1793 and the dishonesty or meanness of the overseers.

During the eighteenth century the parish officers were ordered to provide houses within the village to be used as poor houses, mainly for the aged, sick and those unable to care for themselves. By about 1800, Gotherington had poor houses in Manor Lane and Cleeve Road (Rutley Villa) while Woolstone had strategically built its poor house in Malleson Road (Rhondda Cottage) away from its own village, but for what purpose we do not know.[30] Out-relief in the form of money, rent, and clothing given to those in need but still remaining in their own homes was allowed to the able-bodied, but those whom the authorities decided should enter the poor house would be given no further relief should they refuse to enter.

The poor rate was used for a variety of purposes but chiefly to give relief when no work was available, to support the old and infirm, widows with children to care for, unmarried mothers during their weeks of confinement, and orphans. Rents were paid, coal and wood provided and a variety of items of clothing and bed linen acquired for the needy. Care and clothing were often basic but nonetheless comprehensive. In 1757, for instance, the overseer provided a shirt and shoes for Bevil Blizzard, paid for his washing and lodgings and gave him £3 12s 9d when he had smallpox. Frances Pearton was provided with a gown, coat and two shifts in 1755 and she was receiving weekly pay five years later, shortly before her death. The expenses for her funeral included £3 for the clerk and sexton, £1 for bread and cheese and £3 for beer provided as inducements to her friends to follow the coffin as mourners. The 1775 accounts include an item of £1 17s 6d for the expenses of 'Thos. Mathoses Weding, License, Marrige Ring'. In 1791–2 twenty-three people received relief, representing about one in thirteen of the population, and some would have had dependants also.[31] In a small village the poor could not be hidden or forgotten and on the whole the system seems to have

Rutley Villa in Cleeve Road is now unrecognizable as a building used as a poor house in the eighteenth century

been administered with some kindness and sensitivity, meeting the real immediate needs of the individual.

The Poor Law Act of 1601 in turn gave rise to the law of settlement and removal of 1662, a harsh law which had appalling effects upon the genuine poor. The respectable, hard-working man, unable to find work through no fault of his own, could be prevented from moving in search of work, so becoming a parish pauper forced to accept meagre charity and ending his days in the workhouse. Any man wishing to work away from his parish had to produce a certificate of settlement from his own parish agreeing to take him back if he proved in the future to be a charge on the parish where he took work. No parish accepted such potential liability if it could be avoided, and equally they sought to avoid future commitments for paupers and orphans by apprenticing them in the next parish. In 1754 the vestry minutes record: 'Agreed by the parishioners of the hamlet of Gotherington met in vestry to apprentice out Jane Fowler the first opportunity that offers'.[32]

Removals of those not entitled to settlement in a parish could be complicated and long drawn out, requiring the attendance of the overseer before a magistrate to establish the man's birthplace and life history in terms of jobs held with names and statements from previous employers. A removal order survives from 1743 for the two orphans of John Guy (as there is no mention of a mother one presumes that she was also dead). John Guy had worked and died in Gotherington but had not been granted settlement in the village. His children, Elizabeth aged sixteen and William aged twelve, were proving to be a burden on the community and were being removed to Bishop's Cleeve as this was John Guy's place of settlement, where he had served his appenticeship. Despite the fact that the two villages were part of the same parish the laws of settlement still applied. The family had been the subject of another removal order from Oxenton to Bishop's Cleeve some years previously.[33]

The duties imposed on the unpaid parish officers were clearly onerous and it is not surprising to find that they were carried out with varying skill and care. There were other responsibilities loaded on their shoulders in respect of the moral jurisdiction of the vestry over the parishioners. The churchwardens were required to report evidence of wrongdoing and, depending on the gravity of the offence, the offender would be sentenced by the vestry or sent to the consistory court at Gloucester. The court sat in 1552 before the Bishop of Worcester to consider the case of William Garne who was charged with incontinency with Julian Grining and it was decreed that 'he shall be in the parish church of Cleeve upon Monday come sevennights and bring eight honest men of the sayed parish to purge himself of the crime layd to his charge'. After confessing he was enjoined 'that he shall upon Sunday next at the homily time stand in the parish church of Cleeve and there in his shirte bare headed and bare fote recyte his faults expressed in the sayed [schedule] and likewise upon Sunday comme seven nights at Gloucester in the Cathedrall churche and so upon Sunday next after at Tewkesbury church and so upon the Sunday then next folowinge at the church of Cheltnam and to certify thereof in the consistory of Gloucester.' The other offender failed to attend and was pronounced contumacious and excommunicated. The clear attempt to use the community to punish the accused still reflected the medieval system of law and order. In another case the churchwardens made a presentment of adultery but in a notable display of charity the hearing was postponed for a week because the woman was in childbirth.[34]

THE CHURCH

It will be apparent that the influence exerted on the inhabitants of Gotherington by Bishop's Cleeve church through the vestry was in many respects more powerful than that of the lord of the manor, whose real functions had declined to those of a landlord over his tenants. Rather surprisingly, however, the villagers were apparently left without the benefit of a chapel-of-ease such as those in Stoke Orchard and Southam. After the dispute in the fourteenth century recorded in the previous chapter the only known reference to a chapel in Gotherington occurs in the 1652 survey which includes: '. . . the manor house . . . including an old chapell . . .'[35] but this must have been long disused, as shown by bequests in wills for the benefit of the church at Cleeve and, for example, John Kemmet's will in 1545 in which he left 20*d* 'for mendyng the way as man goith to ye church betwene Gotherington and Cleve'.[36] However, during 1658, in the time of the Commonwealth, an inquiry was held on the subject of 'dividing the hamlet of Gotherington from the parish of Bishop's Cleeve and making it a distinct parish. The patron and incumbent of the parish church and the parishioners and inhabitants of the said parish and hamlett are to have thirty days notice'.[37] (The reader is at liberty to reconstruct the non-existent minutes of the meeting!) There is no evidence that the division was made and, if it was, it would almost certainly have been reversed as soon as the Restoration occurred two years later. Trivial as this event (or non-event) may seem, it is surely of some significance in that the proposal would never have been considered if Gotherington had no building which could have served as its parish church.

J.F. Daubeny has stated that the parish of Bishop's Cleeve had four chapels including those at Stoke Orchard and Southam and one 'in a field on the left of the road from Cleeve to Gotherington of which only the foundations remain, but seventy years ago the key hung in a cottage in Gotherington'.[38] The basis for this claim (made in 1900) is unknown and it seems improbable since no other mention of such a building has been found.

Attendance at the parish church became less universal in the latter part of the period covered in this chapter as Nonconformism began to gain a foothold. An ecclesiastical census in 1676 records thirty-seven dissenters in the parish of Bishop's Cleeve but does not say how many of them were from Gotherington, Southam or Stoke Orchard. There were three in Woolstone, twelve in Oxenton and roughly similar percentages in Cheltenham and Winchcombe, and the numbers would undoubtedly have increased in the religious revival during the eighteenth century.[39] By 1743 it is clear that there were Nonconformist sympathisers in Gotherington because in that year and the next John Wesley held services here and was well received, within the first five years of commencing his open-air ministry.[40]

A PERIOD OF CHANGE

In the period covered in this chapter the way of life in the community was inevitably altered by a number of factors, especially the disappearance of the two manors and the growth of Bishop's Cleeve parish vestry as the real controller of the lives of Gotherington people. But a villager from the sixteenth century might have returned in the first half of the eighteenth century to many familiar scenes. The people worked in the same way, had the same meagre possessions and lived in most cases in familiar thatched, half-timbered cottages. The care of the poor had become institutionalized and secularized as householders had been made to shoulder the responsibility of providing and paying for that care. However, if our villager had returned again at the beginning of the nineteenth century, he would have immediately remarked how the process of change had accelerated. There were some new, well-built farmhouses to catch his eye but the most obvious change was that hedges were springing up where none had been in his day, and the big fields he remembered had all been divided up. It would have taken him some time to understand what had happened at enclosure, which is hardly surprising since it was the biggest single event in the recorded history of the village. Not only was the landscape changed, but the process of land allocation and exchange removed from the poorer labourers their stake in the land. It symbolized the growing gap between the richer and poorer members of the community; a gap which previously had been apparent in the different sizes of land holding, now became absolute and very few labourers would ever be able to take on their own farm from then on.

References

1   J. Thirsk, 'Projects for gentlemen, jobs for the poor; mutual aid in the Vale of Tewkesbury 1600–1630', in *Essays in Bristol and Gloucestershire History*, ed. P. McGrath and J. Cannon (Bristol, 1976), p. 148.

2   *Dictionary of National Biography*, Vol. XIII (London, 1888), p. 43.

3   GRO: D184 M22.

4   GRO: D184 M11; Public Record Office (PRO) C54/375B; Bodleian Library, Oxford (Bod.Lib.), Craven Papers 152, 153.

5   GRO has surveys and rentals as follows:
1540	Ministers' Accounts of Tewkesbury Abbey D2819
1555–63	Gotherington Rental and Court Book D184 M9
1630	Survey D184 M24
1652	Survey D184 M11
1775	Survey D184 P1.

6   In addition to the surveys quoted above, the remaining surveys are:
1552	PRO: KR Miscellaneous Books V39, p. 188
1724	Bod.Lib., Craven Papers 56
1808	GRO: Q/RI 71.

7   GRO: D184 M12.

8   GRO: D184 T61.

9   GRO: D184 M24.

10 GRO: D184 T64.

11 GRO: D184 P1.

12 Bod.Lib.: Craven Papers 37, 38.

13 GRO: AP75.

14 GRO: Q/RI 71.

15 Personal communication.

16 GRO: D184 P1.

17 W. Marshall, *The Rural Economy of Gloucestershire*, Vol. I (1796, reprinted Gloucester, 1979), p. 14.

18 *Transactions of the Bristol and Gloucestershire Archaeological Society*, Vol. 80, pp. 112.

19 GRO: Moore and Son Sale Books, D2080.

20 The relevant turnpike acts are:
1755	29 Geo II c.51
1794	34 Geo III c.135
1818	58 Geo III c.30
1826	7 Geo IV c.78.

21 Local History Pamphlet No. 2, *Wills Proved in Gloucestershire Peculiar Courts* (Gloucester City Libraries, 1960).
22 Gloucester Diocesan Records (GDR) in GRO: Bishop's Cleeve Peculiar, Inventory 15.
23 Loc. cit. Will 18.
24 Loc. cit. Will 2.
25 GDR: Gloucestershire Wills 1762, 129.
26 J.S. Moore, *Goods and Chattels of our Forefathers* (London and Chichester, 1976), p. 35.
27 J. Smith, *Men and Armour for Gloucestershire in 1608* (reprinted Gloucester, 1980), pp. 105–6.
28 GRO: D383.
29 GRO: P46 VE and OV series.
30 GRO: Q/RI 71.
31 GRO: P46 OV2/2.
32 GRO: P46 VE1/1.
33 Ibid.
34 GCL: *Hockaday Abstracts*, Vol. 159, 1552, 1572.
35 GRO: D184 M11.
36 GCL: *Hockaday Abstracts*, Vol. 160, 1545.
37 Lambeth Palace Library, MS991, fo. 471.
38 J.F. Daubeny, *Cleeve Common, Glos., Rights and Regulations over the Common* (London, 1900), p. 97.
39 GRO: Compton Census, photocopy 377.
40 J. Wesley, *Journals*, 13 October 1743, 8 May 1744.

CHAPTER SEVEN

The Links with the Past Begin to Break

Gotherington 1808–96

Hilda Bishop and Eunice Powell

In the nineteenth century the villagers of Gotherington remained overwhelmingly dependent upon agriculture, yet at both ends of the century great changes took place. In 1807 enclosure had remade the fields, in 1894 the Craven's manor, descendant of the medieval manor of Upper Gotherington, was sold off, and for the first time in recorded history the land of the community was largely in the hands of people who lived there.

Little information exists on the last half-century of the long reign of the Cravens as lords of the Gotherington manor, before they sold it to James Hutchinson of Cheltenham in 1853. The rent lists for 1801 to 1807 show large increases over the rents in the early eighteenth century when all tenants except one paid less than £2 a year and the total annual rent was under £25 a year.[1] After the creation of some larger units as described in the previous chapter and the increasing prosperity of the farmers resulting from rising food prices, the Cravens were able to increase their income from the manor. The total annual rent had risen to £680 in 1801 and was to double again by 1807 – the year of enclosure. The larger farms now paid up to £300 whereas the rents charged for cottages remained unchanged at 1s or 2s 6d. Unfortunately no rent lists appear to have survived from 1808 to 1851 but there is one for 1852, the last year before the manor was sold. The total was 10 per cent less than that for 1807, evidence of the increasing unattractiveness of the manor for the Craven family and the main factor in their decision to sell.

In 1851 the various Craven properties appear to have remained entities but not so all the freehold properties. Part of the arable land of Hales Farm had been sold to George Ruddle who let it as allotments. White's, otherwise Lawrence's, Farm appears to have remained intact but with additions. However, the very large estate in Gotherington and elsewhere which John Nind of Home Farm had built up in his lifetime was split up after his death in 1808 among his children and grandchildren. In 1851 his descendants were occupying at least seven dwellings in Gotherington, and the widowers of three of his grandchildren another three. Two of his granddaughters, Sarah Fisher and Susannah Cresswell were still farming after the death of their husbands. Sarah had the larger part as she had inherited a sixth share of her father William Nind's estate and that of her first husband John Nind who had been her cousin. Another granddaughter, Elizabeth, inherited the land on the east of Evesham Road on which her husband John Perry built the Farmers' Arms in 1833.[2] Was the pond there the result of digging clay for bricks? John Perry also farmed fifteen acres. Despite the large size of the Nind family and its extensive possessions, the name has disappeared from the village today, although descendants through the female side are still living in the village. The number of present families who can trace their name back to these years is very few, but not surprising given the mobility of people in the past.

Hales Farm was a freeholding in Lower Gotherington

It was also in 1833 that a place for Nonconformist worship was built in Gotherington after applications to the Bishop of Gloucester from the farmers and others for his sanction of meetings for such worship in the village. The Reverend Norman Lloyd has written a full history called *Gotherington Free Church 1833–1983*.[3] This was the first place of worship to be built in the village since the decay of the medieval chapel-at-ease near the manor-house. There seems to have been a continuous history of Methodism in Gotherington since the visits of John Wesley recorded in the previous chapter, and three applications were made to the bishop to hold Nonconformist services in various houses before the Craven family gave a plot of land for a permanent chapel. In these early years, the congregation was connected to Cheltenham chapel (now offices by the bowling green in the Lower High Street) and the chapel at Woodmancote, all part of the Countess of Huntingdon's Connexion. Fifty people attended the chapel on census Sunday in March 1851.

The township of Gotherington was still in the parish of Bishop's Cleeve and continued to be subject to the authority of the vestry. Most of its inhabitants, including chapel-goers, were baptized, married and buried at St Michael's church in Bishop's Cleeve but some with family connections went to St Martin's, Woolstone. It was not until 1933 that Gotherington became part of the ecclesiastical parish of Woolstone with Oxenton.

THE TREATMENT OF THE POOR

As the village continued throughout the century as a part of Bishop's Cleeve parish it was still therefore subject to the authority of the vestry. There was no great wealth in the community and most people lived in danger of becoming dependent upon poor relief for support in sickness, infirmity or old age. This was in the days before modern benefits. The poor continued to be immobilized by the laws of settlement and removal, as they had been during the eighteenth century, and were penalized by the acts of enclosure when common rights of

Home Farm was another holding based on the medieval manor of Lower Gotherington. In the late eighteenth century John Nind built it into a large farm holding which lasted until only shortly after his death

pasture were exchanged for small pieces of poorish land, not large enough to graze their animals, as recorded in the previous chapter.

The vestry minutes and overseers' accounts for Gotherington during the early years show little change from the previous century in the items which were dealt with, except that more people were needing relief of some kind. Farm workers' pay in the early years of the nineteenth century was roughly £8 to £12 a year and that of domestic servants anything from £3 to £12 a year according to the status and class of employer.

The overseers' accounts for 1808–9 are typical for those years.[4] They show that relief was allowed for differing periods, two weeks to fifty weeks, and recipients were being paid anything from 1s 3d a week to 5s a week, depending on circumstances: sickness, unemployment, age and infirmity, family to provide for or widowed. Individual items were handed out to needy villagers. The same accounts show that shoes, coats, mutton, coal and wood were all handed out during the year. Visits to the doctor were paid for, as were funeral expenses for paupers and the washing of bed linen. The overseers paid the Bridge Money (Gotherington's part of the cost of upkeep of several bridges shared with other villages) and handed out money for sparrows caught (sparrows were classed as vermin). Two items of £14 12s 6d and £6 15s 0d paid to the overseers of Cheltenham and Stonehouse could well have been relief for Gotherington residents living, but not legally settled, in these places.

The accounts for 1810/11 included the following:

Pd Mary Valinder for helping to lay out Jane Wilks	3s 0d
Pd for the Shroud for Jane Wilks	5s 0d
Pd for Bell and Grave for ditto	6s 0d
Pd for Bread and Cheese and Beer for ditto	17s 0d

A pauper's death was not necessarily a cheap and undignified ending at this time. In a parish where everyone knew everyone else the body was decently dealt with and mourners would attend even if persuaded by the dole of bread, cheese and beer as indicated in the accounts. One can imagine the burial party and coffin slowly making their way across the fields to Bishop's Cleeve along the path running from Shutter Lane.[5]

In the same accounts the overseer spent over £5 on matters concerning James Cresswell's trial, although we are not told his crime. The money was spent visiting at least four inns in the locality, possibly pursuing witnesses.

Pd at the Old Bear Inn in Gloucester concerning James Cresswell's trial	17s 7d
Pd at the Public when James Cresswell was taken to Oxenton	£1 8s 6d
Pd at the Lamb Inn concerning James Cresswell's trial	7s 8d
Pd at the Black Dog Inn Gloucester concerning James Cresswell's trial	£3 0s 6d

Such a payment made quite a hole in the amounts available to give out to the poor.

Several accounts have references to William Valinder and his family needing relief of some sort or another but two items in the accounts of 1820 highlight a sad occurrence:

Pd Samuel Reeves for fetching the Corner [i.e. coroner] two [i.e. to] William Valinder's child	3s 0d
Pd 12 Jury men 8d each for a tending [i.e. attending] on a Corner's inquest on William Valinder's child which was burned to death	8s 0d
[The child, Thomas, was buried on 23 April aged 1]	

The same accounts include: 'Expenses at Cheltenham for Bering Hopkins Child £1 3s 0d' and four other references to children being ill. They remind us that in a pauper's household it was the children who often succumbed to the harshness of life.

Children born outside a marriage and claims against a known father remained within the province of the overseers, and the accounts show expenses for swearing out summons against these men, a very necessary task if the township of Gotherington was not to bear the cost of the child. Amounts received from other parishes for women and children would seem to indicate that claims of this nature were often successful.

A reference in the accounts of 1828/9, 'making a return of the luniticks – 0 2s 6d' shows that these people also came under the care of the overseers. Indeed from 1819 to 1836 over a period of seventeen years the overseers spent over £500 on the care and welfare of one villager, John Brown, who was probably mentally unstable and was confined for part of the time at Droitwich, possibly in the asylum.[6]

The men who served in the office of overseer were appointed for a year at a time and were all villagers; the people they were dealing with were those well known to them and indeed possibly related to them. However difficult and harsh the life of the paupers and despite, no doubt, the occasional mean and unscrupulous overseer, relief came from within the family of the village. Ratepayers might grumble but all expected to pay for their own poor. This is why the laws of settlement and removal were so strictly adhered to. Paying for one's own poor was a fact of life, paying for someone else's poor was to be avoided at all costs.

A good run of papers recording the examination of paupers survive for Cheltenham for 1815–26.[7] They include a number of people who had claimed relief from Gotherington. The examinations were taken in front of magistrates to decide whether the examinants were entitled to receive it: did they in fact have, or had they acquired, legal settlement in Gotherington, or should they be given relief in some other village? The following examples give us some idea of how people came to fall into poverty at that time. They also provide further evidence on how much people moved around in the past.

9 May 1815 John Brown
'Born at Gotherington in Bishop's Cleeve where his parents were settled, they having received relief from the overseers there. Has been hired into several services since he was emancipated from his father but never for a full year. For the last 10 or 12 years has been a soldier or sailor, but for the last three quarters of a year has been at Sheffield, Yorks., where he married Elizabeth his present wife, now residing with him.'[8]

20 May 1817 Philip Burbridge
'Born in Toddington. When young he was appointed to Robert Harris of Gotherington for seven years. Being at that time very wild, he frequently ran away from his master's service but always returned and his master received him; but about three months before the seven years were expired he agreed to leave his master altogether and his master consented thereto on receiving four guineas.'[9]

22 July 1823 Betty Hemming
'Born in Gotherington and has never done any act to gain a settlement.'

Mary Hemming
'Her daughter Betty was born in wedlock. Her husband who is now dead received relief from the parish of Woolstone and she now resides in a house belonging to the officers of that parish.'[10]

It is not known whether the John Brown mentioned here is the same man who received relief from Gotherington from 1819 to 1826 but it seems likely. The case of Philip Burbridge shows that although apprenticeship could help to establish settlement it was necessary to complete the full seven years. The case of Mary Hemming and her daughter Betty was no doubt a dispute between Woolstone and Gotherington, made more interesting because she was actually living in Gotherington; the present Rhondda Cottage being Woolstone's poor house as explained in the previous chapter.

During the nineteenth century it was the poor whose names occur in the records of crime. The poor man's life was hedged around with restrictions and laws, an infringement of which brought swift and often severe punishment. Gotherington had its share of criminals, mainly petty thieves, who would serve their sentences in Gloucester or Northleach prisons. It is known that two Gotherington men were sentenced to be transported to Australia for their crimes. They were both charged with theft, John Lane, aged thirty-seven, for stealing a quantity of plates and dishes from Anthony Webb of Bishop's Cleeve in 1832, and William Barnett for stealing an iron cart arm from John Brooks of Bishop's Cleeve in 1835.[11]

William Barnett had been charged at the age of twenty-one with having stolen from James Roberts, possibly a near neighbour in Gotherington, a silver watch, a quantity of clothing, bread and bacon. For this he received eighteen months in gaol. For his second offence in 1835 he was transported for seven years.[12] John Lane, along with his brother Henry Lane, had also previously been charged in 1826 with stealing two bushels of apples from John New of Dixton but on this occasion had been found not guilty. The later offence in 1832 brought the death sentence which was commuted to transportation for life. These were the usual punishments for such crimes in an age when harsh penalties were meted out as deterrents in the absence of a professional police force (which did not appear in Gloucestershire for another quarter of a century). The noteworthiness of these two isolated cases illustrates, of course, the basically law-abiding nature of the village community in these years.

An interesting sidelight on these crimes is that we have a detailed description of both men from the Register of Prisoners. William Barnett stood 5 ft 6 in tall with dark hair, grey eyes, a round face with fair complexion, light sandy whiskers and a scar on his right arm. He was a labourer and could read but not write. John Lane was a smaller man, 5 ft 4$\frac{1}{2}$ in tall, with dark brown hair and dark grey eyes. He had a brown complexion, long face, long nose and two small moles on his right cheek, and scars on his left hand and back. He too was a labourer and could not read. Both men were sent to Van Dieman's Land (Tasmania), Lane leaving behind a wife and family. There is no record that Barnett ever returned.

Gotherington's history can never be isolated from the wider world. In 1834 the New Poor Law was passed by parliament. The act forced parishes to amalgamate into unions and to elect guardians from each parish to govern the new union and its workhouse. Gotherington became part of Winchcombe Union and the poor of the village were no longer the direct concern of the village. Although the poorhouses within the village continued to be used from some time, the new union workhouse was built in Winchcombe. The poor rate continued to be levied and was collected by the village overseer on behalf of the union. The main importance of the new act was that it was much more concerned with the interests of the rate-payers rather than with the needs of the poor and poverty began to be regarded as somehow the fault of the poor, to be punished harshly as a crime.

Out-relief (paupers receiving rent and allowances but remaining in their own houses) continued for some time but the aged and infirm and chronically ill were sent to the workhouse in Winchcombe. However enlightened the master of the workhouse it was still a harsh system. The sexes were usually segregated in order that no more dependants should be born and this division broke up many happy families. The Winchcombe Master's Journals refer on several occasions to vagrants requesting overnight lodging.[13] On being shown the accommodation and bedding provided they preferred to move on, one man stating he would walk all night rather than stay in such conditions! Above all it was the lack of respect and personal freedom that the common people feared. Centuries of community help for its own poor were ended by an act imposed on the people of Gotherington from outside, and in which they had little or no say, for only a tiny fraction of the population had a vote for a member of parliament.

THE HOMES OF THE VILLAGERS

Much of our information about the lives of the people of Gotherington in the early part of the nineteenth century comes from wills, inventories, indentures and parish registers, many of which can be seen at the Gloucestershire Record Office.

The will made in 1803 by Mary Jordan, the widow of William Jordan at Baldwin's Farm, gives us an excellent idea of the personal possessions of a farmer's wife with a holding of twenty-seven acres.[14] She left £30 to John Dobbins of Clifton Ashchurch for the maintenance and upbringing of her 'natural' daughter Ann and also left to Ann (aged sixteen) 'two gowns, two linen and two woollen aprons, my best white apron and handkerchief, my best cap and two cloaks, my best black quilt petticoat, all my shifts, my best pair of stays and one tablecloth, one pair of sheets, the best bed quilt, one bed and an oak chest of drawers and the curtains and hangings of the bed on which I lie; two ironhooped hogsheads which were my brother Leech's, five silver tea spoons marked with the initials of my said daughter's name and a pair of silver tea tongs marked in like manner, and gold ring that was my mother's, two brass candlesticks and my spice mortar and pestle, six pewter plates and four dishes, also the bedstead on which I lie and my wooden teaboard for the sole and absolute use of my said daughter Ann Leech.' (Ann married John Rose at Bishop's Cleeve church five years later in 1808).[15] Mary Jordan left 'the rest of my real estate and stock to my good friend Giles Perry upon trust for the benefit of my five children by my husband William Jordan for their maintenance, education, apprenticeship – Giles Perry to be their guardian, John Dobbins to advise them and my sister Elizabeth Leech to befriend them.'

The Land Tax list of 1791 provides the clue that Mary's husband had been sharing Baldwin's Farm with her brother William Leech.[16] Both her husband and her brother had died in 1802 and there was an auction of Mrs Jordan's 'Farm Stock and Implements of Husbandry' by Moore's of Tewkesbury on 17 May 1803, four days after she made her will, arranged presumably for her by Giles Perry whom she had named executor and to whom the auctioneer handed the profits of £132 11s 2d.[17] The record of the auction provides us with an excellent snapshot of the equipment of a small farm in the early nineteenth century:

1. Cart Mare – Jewell, 2. Bay Horse – Sharper, 3. Brown Horse – Captain, 4. Black Mare – Flower, 5. One Pony, 6. One Milch Cow, 7. One Heifer in Calf, 8. One Milch Cow and calf, 9. One Sow and seven Pigs.

10. One Waggon, 11. Another, 12. One narrow wheel cart, 13. One broad wheel cart, 14. One Plough and Wheel, 15. One Plough and Dray, 16. One Pair of Harrows, 17. Another pair, 18. Barley roll, 19. Cow Crib and Waggon Jack.

20. One set of long Geering, 21, 22, 23, 24. Four more sets, 25. One Set Tillers Geering, 26. Quantity of Boltins, 27. Two Corn Skreens, 28. One Half Hogshead, 29, 30, 31. Three more, 32. Quantity of Odd Geering, 33. Four Horse ties, 34. Cheese Rack, 35. Long Ladder, 36. Short Ladder, 37. Winnowing fan, 38. Chaff Box, 39. Three Sheppikes and one Rake, 40. One Stone Pigs Trough, 41. Two Wood Pigs Troughs, 42. One Cart Rope, 43. A Wheat and Bean Rick, 44. Seven Stone Staddles, 45. Seven more. 46. Quantity of bags, 47. Four sieves.

Here were the furniture and equipment that we would expect from a small tenant farm. The wealth of the farm lay in the stock and farm equipment. Horses were used for traction, the cows kept for the Jordans' own diary needs, similarily the one sow and seven piglets. The equipment clearly suggests an arable farm and it is interesting to note the stone staddles for raising the granary off the ground. One can almost imagine Mary Jordan in her black petticoat and white apron busying around Baldwin's Farm, milking cows, making cheese, feeding the pigs and organizing the farm labourers in their work in the fields. Such domestic detail adds greatly to our understanding of the village in the past.

One of the changes that was taking place in the village during the early nineteenth century was a general increase in the standard of living, although by our criteria, even that of the richest villagers would be considered rather poor. Villagers who felt they possessed a quantity of possessions sometimes had them valued. In 1843 Hannah Harris had an inventory drawn up of her furniture and effects by local farmer Richard Williams and John Moore of Tewkesbury.[18] Hannah was the widow of Robert Harris whose family of cordwainers, or shoemakers, had owned Cotswold Cottage in Shutter Lane for about a hundred years, and mother of Charlotte Harris, shopkeeper and owner of a certain amount of land. It appears that the cordwainers had invested their profits in purchasing land, as did the maltsters next door. Their status would have been in the middle between the farmers and the agricultural labourers. As the same family had inhabited the same house for so long there would have been time for household goods to accumulate.

In Hannah Harris's kitchen there were: two brass candlesticks, two iron candlesticks and a tinder-box, fender steel and (?), a fire shovel and tongs, brass (litpad?), bellows and a chopping knife, box iron, fire links and a fender, a copper tea kettle, salt coffer, bacon rack, oak pillar table, folding screen, seven ash chairs, oak dresser and shelves, a brass pepper box, sitting screen, hanging glass, oak corner cupboard, tea chinas, and silver teaspoons. In the drinkhouse (where the drink was kept) were three half hogsheads, a quarter barrel, wine cask, square cupboard, small cask and bottle, two shelves and hanging shelf, and two (illegible). In the chambers or bedrooms were a four-post bedstead, check furniture, an oak chest of drawers, dressing glass, an oak dressing table, coffer and box, night stool, oak post bedstead, two feather beds and bolsters, another bed and bolster, oak linen chest, coffer and two boxes and a bench. In the shop were an empty pipe, quarter barrer, coffer and pepper mills, table, oval brass pot, five canisters, nest of drawers, counter, and ironing board. Elsewhere were a cowl, four dry casks, mash tub, bench and iron furnace hanging. The total value was £23.

Hannah Harris was clearly not poor. The poorer people have not left any record of their limited possessions which must have been passed on to the next generation without any need to record the transaction. Unfortunately for historians the majority of the families fell into this category.

Who Were the People in Gotherington?

The census of 1851 makes this a good year in which to consider the make-up of the population of Gotherington, as it gives information which can be checked against a Poor Rate List of the same year giving the names of both owners and occupiers of the properties with the total acreage of each.[19] There were five large farms of over one hundred acres. Of these the largest was Tithe Farm, 295 acres in Gotherington Fields, at the extreme west of Gotherington, owned by the Rector of Bishop's Cleeve and occupied by John Cooke. The Craven estate owned the other four large farms:

Manor Farm	282 acres occupied by	John Fowler
Moat Farm	159 acres occupied by	John Holder
Yew Tree Farm	130 acres occupied by	William Hobbs
Brick House Farm	119 acres occupied by	William Jackson
and also		
Laurel Farm	70 acres occupied by	John Taylor
Truman's Farm	54 acres occupied by	James Hobbs

The freehold farms were smaller. All except Baldwin's Farm were still based on the medieval freeholdings of Lower Gotherington. Baldwin's had been part of medieval Upper Gotherington.

Home Farm	51 acres owned by	Mrs Sarah Fisher
Lawrence's/White's	51 acres owned by	George Hone
Baldwin's Farm	27 acres owned by	Richard Fowler
Hales Farm	25 acres owned by	William Harman

In total there were seventeen identifiable farm holdings.

The census provides a picture of a village totally dependent upon agriculture. The total population of the parish was 424; of these, 125 men, women and children were described as agricultural labourers, but the census also reveals that there were only regular jobs for eighty-nine of them in the parish, so some would have travelled for regular work. The village had become over-populated because there were too few jobs for its potential workers, but despite this only thirteen people were classed as paupers, who depended entirely on the poor law for support. They were all aged, and today they would all be drawing a pension. Another measure of the dependence upon agriculture was that fifty-four of the ninety-four separate households held at least one agricultural labourer. Six people were described as farm servants. This was a traditional method of ensuring the farmer had sufficient labour, but it was fast disappearing in the mid-nineteenth century, as farmers preferred to hire their workers rather than provide them with board and lodging.

Another noticeable feature of Gotherington in 1851 was the number of children: 145 under the age of fifteen, over a third of the total population. There were children everywhere. Many were described as agricultural labourers, including one girl of five, presumably because she could not be left at home in the house. Only eighteen children were described as scholars; the impact of mass education still lay in the future, but many children probably learnt to read and write at Sunday school. Parents could not afford the double burden of paying for their children to attend day-school and thus foregoing the income from their meagre wages.

Even those people who did not directly work in agriculture depended upon it indirectly. The craftsmen and their families are the best example. The major crafts were those of the stonemasons (the Pearts) and the wheelwrights and carpenters (the Wymans and their employees). There is a farm wagon built by the Wymans in a museum in Bristol and a plough made by William Wyman in the Welsh Folk Museum at St Fagan's, near Cardiff. Their premises were just outside the village along Cleeve Road. There were four blacksmiths (the Sollises in Cleeve Road and the Cresswells in Shutter Lane) one tailor, three dressmakers, three cordwainers, or shoemakers, with an apprentice, one victualler (William Reeve of the Shutter Inn), one maltster (George Reeve of the Malt Shovel in Shutter Lane), two grocers (Mrs Priscilla Clarke at Ekia in Gretton Road and Miss Charlotte Harris at Cotswold Cottage in Shutter Lane), also a lodging house keeper, four housekeepers, eight domestic servants, a nurse and a monthly nurse, a schoolmaster (Samuel Lye) and a schoolmistress (Jane Lawrence) to teach the eighteen scholars. There were four landed proprietors.

The village was quite typical of a medium sized agricultural community. Although the Craven family was the largest landowner, the village lacked a resident family in a great house, for the Cravens had extensive estates across the country. This lack of a resident lord can be seen reflected in the small number of domestic servants. Gotherington was a more uniform community with no very rich people and only thirteen described as paupers.

The Firs in Malleson Road is typical of the houses built during the first half of the nineteenth century as Gotherington expanded

The last traditional village craft to survive was the baker's. Price's bakery was attached to Ivy Cottage in Gretton Road, built by Joseph Peart and a good example of the larger houses built in Gotherington in the nineteenth century

Power lay in the hands of the larger farmers on whom the large number of agricultural labourers depended for their livelihood. There had been no real change in the traditional basis of the community's economy – agriculture – but dependence on just one industry made the village vulnerable to agricultural change which hit the farmlands in the third quarter of the nineteenth century.

Until 1851 the population had been steadily growing. New homes had been built for the inhabitants and we know many of those were built in the first half of the nineteenth century. In addition to the Farmers' Arms and the Free church, the following new houses were built in the first half of the nineteenth century: Stone House in Malleson Road, built presumably by John and James Reeve, carpenters and wheelwrights, between 1809 and 1825 for their widowed mother. It is built on a very stout timber-framing with lathe and plaster inner walls and a stone facing outside. Other houses included, in the Granna Lane area, Cotswold Vale for Thomas Barnard, and Prescott Cottage, now known as The Folly, for J.F. Peacey; on the east side of Evesham Road, a farmhouse for William Robinson, demolished in the twentieth century; on the north side of Malleson Road, Shill Cottage, now known as The Firs for the landed proprietor John Shill; on the east side of Shill Cottage, a cottage for Thomas Etherington from Nottingham, a house and land proprietor; a cottage which forms part of 110 Malleson Road and a cottage demolished when 112 Malleson Road was built.

The most distinguished of the new buildings in the second half of the nineteenth century were built by Joseph Peart, son of Isaac Peart, a stonemason, who came originally from the Worcester area: Ivy Cottage the house to which the former bakery in Gretton Road is attached (the first inhabitant was Catherine Willis, the schoolmistress); Long Furlong Cottage, built for Mrs Sarah Fisher; Gotherington Board School which was opened in 1883, and The Holt in Cleeve Road which Joseph Peart built for himself and his new wife. The Pearts demolished three medieval houses to form the grounds of The Holt.

The Holt

THE VILLAGE GOES INTO DECLINE

The prosperity represented by this building did not last. In the middle of the nineteenth century, landlords faced a decision at a time of greater demands for more food and with the threat of cheap food imports: spend capital to introduce improved methods of farming (machinery, efficient drainage, etc.) or leave the farms to become uncompetitive. The Cravens must have concluded that there were more worthwhile investments to be made in the developing industries, and they were proved right about twenty years later when even the more efficient farms began to encounter severe competition from grain imports from America and Canada, and later cheap refrigerated meat shipments from Argentina and New Zealand.

When the Right Honourable Henry Augustus Berkeley Craven, then owner of the Craven estates, died in 1853, his nephew and heir, the Right Honourable William Earl of Craven decided to sell the Gotherington estate. Although the *Gloucester Journal* carried notices of the sale by auction of 'several eligible farms, cottages and gardens' to be held in May 1853 it appears that the whole estate must have been sold privately to the new lord of the manor, James Hutchinson of Cheltenham.[20] James Hutchinson added to the estate the freehold Baldwin's Farm after the death of its owner Richard Fowler in September 1858. His son added the orchard in Manor Lane on the end of which Brick House Cottage was built and later his grandson acquired the tiny one-up one-down cottage in Cleeve Road opposite Rutley Villa.

With the imports of cheap grain from overseas in the latter part of the nineteenth century, arable farming became less profitable and one result seems to have been the planting of more

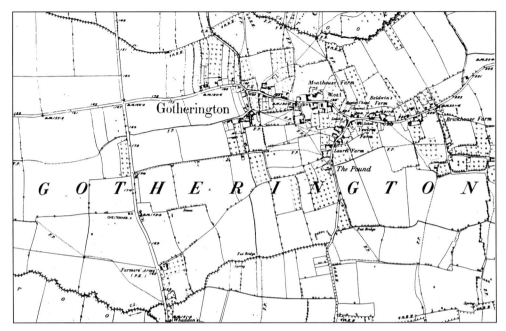

The 1884 six inch Ordnance Survey map recorded the shape of the settlement in the final years of its long life as a community wholly dependent upon agriculture

orchards. There were forty-six orchards on the 1884 map of Gotherington while only sixteen were mentioned in the Enclosure Awards. These orchards would have provided not only grazing for animals but fruit for the Cheltenham market as well as apples and pears for the local cider mills, often mentioned in wills, to make their cider and perry. Some of the little wooden cider kegs which the agricultural labourers took with them into the fields are still in the possession of their descendants. Also in the 1881 census appear eight 'domestic gardeners' presumably growing vegetables for the town.[21] Elderly people in the 1950s remembered the women of Gotherington walking along the Evesham Road into Cheltenham to sell their butter and eggs. This road between Bishop's Cleeve and Cheltenham was deturnpiked in 1880, the earlier turnpike northwards of Bishop's Cleeve having already been deturnpiked in 1877.[22]

A result of the developments in agricultural machinery was that fewer agricultural labourers were required. By the time of the census of 1881 the population had fallen by thirty-six. Only four women (other than poulterers or butterdealers) and no children were listed as agricultural labourers. There is an increase in the number of dressmakers and domestic or general servants, but otherwise the make up of the population is about the same.

Children who in earlier censuses were described as agricultural labourers, now went to school. The census lists Mrs Catherine Willis and Jane Lawrence as schoolmistresses – presumably of a private school – and seventy-seven children under the age of twelve, and nineteen aged twelve and over are listed as scholars, a great change since 1851. Gotherington Board School was opened on 18 July 1881 and only thirty-four children arrived on the first day though the number rose to seventy by the last day of the short term (10 August), as Owen Stinchcombe tells us in his very complete history of the school, *Lucky to Survive*.[23]

The link between agricultural prosperity and decline, and the village population, is very clear, as the decennial census figures show:[24]

Gotherington Academy.

The Inhabitants of Gotherington and the neighbourhood, are respectfully informed that

MR. RADFORD,

is about to commence a SCHOOL, at the newly-erected Villa, opposite the Brick House Farm, where a sound English Education may be obtained, together with a full knowledge of Writing, Arithmetic, English and Scripture History, and Geography.

Especial attention will be given to the moral training of the Scholars.

TERMS: 15s. PER QUARTER.—LATIN, FRENCH, DRAWING, &c. EXTRA.

A Quarter's Notice before removal of a Pupil required.

School will commence (D.V.) on July 17th.

Gotherington, July 1st, 1862.

We know little about this early venture to educate the children of Gotherington, but it was hardly likely to attract the children of agricultural labourers

1801	1811	1821	1831	1841	1851	1861	1871	1881	1891	1901
335	348	348	373	381	424	387	408	388	364	334

An interesting aspect of population which is hidden by these figures is the amount of immigration and emigration. From 1841 to 1901 each census gives evidence of around half the population having moved in or out every ten years. This is clearly contrary to the generally held idea that people never moved around in the past. It is also the reason why no family recorded in the 1851 census still lives with unbroken succession in the village today. Significantly this percentage figure is very similar to that in the present village, despite the village's great expansion as will be outlined in Chapter 9. Another measure of the decline of agriculture is reflected in the rateable value of the village. According to Kelly's Directories this was also going down: £2,890 in 1870, £3,311 in 1879, £2,479 in 1887, £2,286 in 1889, £2,072 in 1897, £2,094 in 1906.[25] It is also significant that the total annual rent of the manor in 1894 was £835 compared to £1,230 in 1852 and £1,370 in 1807.

The decline of agricultural fortunes showed no sign of coming to an end. The rural population was falling even though the national population was doubling between 1841 and 1901, and there is no evidence that anything had been done to improve the local economy. By the end of the nineteenth century, agriculture which had been the backbone of the community's economy and livelihood throughout recorded history, was in terminal decline. This decline led to the break-up of the landholding pattern which had existed for a thousand years since before the Norman Conquest. The year 1894 marks a turning point in the history of Gotherington, as great as those in the late tenth century, when it was split from Bishop's Cleeve; or in the sixteenth century with the dissolution of Tewkesbury Abbey; or even enclosure in 1807. Two events mark the end of the old order and the beginning of the new.

GLOUCESTERSHIRE,

About 4½ miles from the Town of Cheltenham, an important market centre; 6 miles from the famous old Town of Tewkesbury; 4 miles from Ashchurch, with its Station on the Midland Railway; and 2½ miles from Cleeve Station (Midland Railway).

PARTICULARS, PLANS AND CONDITIONS OF SALE OF

VERY VALUABLE

FREEHOLD PROPERTY,

COMPRISING THE

GOTHERINGTON ESTATE,

All lying within the Hamlet of Gotherington, in the Parish of Bishop's Cleeve, and intersected by a main road from Cheltenham to Winchcomb. It includes

VARIOUS-SIZED AGRICULTURAL HOLDINGS,

Each with good FARM HOUSE and ample HOMESTEAD attached,

SEVERAL EXCELLENT SMALL HOLDINGS, ACCOMMODATION LANDS AND A NUMBER OF COTTAGES,

Constituting the greater part of

GOTHERINGTON VILLAGE,

Divided into convenient Lots to suit the requirements of both large and small buyers, and forming

CAPITAL INVESTMENTS.

The Estate for the most part lies well together, and includes some

THRIVING WOODLAND,

With a thick undergrowth capable of holding a good head of Pheasants; in addition to which the higher ground affords capital Rough Shooting.

THE WHOLE EXTENDS OVER AN AREA OF ABOUT

914 ACRES,

Having a total Rental Value, after considerable reductions to meet the depressed times, of

£853 PER ANNUM:

FOR SALE BY AUCTION, IN TWENTY-ONE LOTS, BY

Messrs. OSBORN & MERCER,

AT THE PLOUGH HOTEL, CHELTENHAM,

On THURSDAY, the 22nd of NOVEMBER, 1894,

AT 1.30 FOR 2 O'CLOCK TO THE MINUTE.

Particulars, with Plans and Conditions of Sale, may be obtained of Messrs. SHARPE, PARKER, PRITCHARDS & BARHAM, Solicitors, 12, New Court, Carey Street, London, W.C.; of Mr. JOHN G. VILLAR, Land Agent, 8, Clarence Street, Cheltenham; and of the AUCTIONEERS,

Albemarle House, 28b, Albemarle Street, Piccadilly, London, W.

VACHER & SONS, Printers, Westminster.

4 K

In the harsh times of the 1890s the Craven estate was broken up for the sale in 1894. The last farm was not sold until 1905 (G. Gilder)

THE END OF THE MANOR

In 1894 James Hutchinson, grandson of the 1853 purchaser, decided to sell the whole of his Gotherington estate. The estate of 914 acres, presumably because there was no hope of finding a purchaser for the whole, was put for auction in twenty-one lots at the Plough Hotel, Cheltenham by Messrs. Osborn and Mercer on 22 November 1894.[26] Some lots were considered suitable for small buyers. These were the small cottages occupied mostly by agricultural labourers. In the sale catalogue details of each cottage or other property are given. The small cottages generally consisted of two rooms up and two rooms down, a wash-house outside with boiler attached, a closet in the garden and often a pigsty. When the cottages were semi-detached the outside facilities were sometimes shared. They were mostly stone or brick and stone, with thatched or tiled roofs.

Originally the cottages had depended on their wells for water. The Hutchinsons had constructed a reservoir on the slope of Nottingham Hill behind Manor Farm and piped the water to supply almost all the houses on their estate at an annual rate of five shillings to the cottages and higher prices to the farmers and bigger users. A few who had exceptionally good wells continued to use them. The part of the village which had not formed part of the Craven estate continued to use the wells until mains water was brought to the village. When selling, the Hutchinsons reserved their water rights and rights of entry to maintain the water pipes across the lands where they lay.

The farmhouses were substantial buildings, stone built except for the newest, Brick House Farm. The farm buildings added over many years varied in material according to the period in which they were constructed. Details of the tenants given in the sale catalogue show that certain changes had been taking place in the management of the farms. Like his predecessors, James Hutchinson was an absentee landowner. He had a land agent, Mr John G. Villar, and parts of Manor Farm (Lot 1) were let to three different farmers and a sportsman. Three parts of the land of Yew Tree Farm were let to different farmers (Lot 13) and so on. Only half the lots were sold in 1894 and only one of these was a sizeable farm (Moat Farm, eighty-nine acres). The other four large farms failed to sell and the rest of the lots attracting a buyer were all either a cottage or a pair of cottages or a cottage site or an orchard, except for Truman's Farm which at that time had only fifteen acres of land. The prices expected to be reached for the large farms were apparently over twenty times the annual rental, and potential purchasers must have had doubts whether the current levels of rent could be maintained. Paying £160 for a cottage and orchard let for £8 10s was one thing, paying nearly £3,000 for Yew Tree Farm with an annual rent of £132 was a more serious matter. Another sale was held in 1895. Here, of thirteen rearranged lots, seven were sold but the largest single lot (Manor Farm and three hundred acres) failed to go, as did Baldwin's Farm. This only found a buyer in 1905 when it was bought by John Cooke of Shurdington, at a lower price.

So ended the manor after a thousand years of history, leaving only names in the landscape. The medieval division into Upper and Lower Gotherington survived almost into our own day, although the active use of the two terms had long ceased to be current. Despite land transactions since the mid-sixteenth century, the Craven estate still largely reflected the extent of Upper Gotherington. As long as traditional agriculture formed the basis of the village's economy the historic divisions in the village kept a meaning. It is no coincidence that these divisions disappeared when agriculture suffered its late-nineteenth century decline.

1894 also brought another break with the past, at the same time as it heralded in the new. The local government link with Bishop's Cleeve was broken. A Local Government Act was passed and every village numbering three hundred or more inhabitants was obliged to elect its own parish council. Gotherington ceased to be part of the civil parish of Bishop's Cleeve although it remained part of the ecclesiastical parish till 1933. No longer did it rely for its government on the vestry meeting in Bishop's Cleeve; it now had its own parish council and a new chapter in its history began.

References

1   The rental books are in the Craven estate papers in the Gloucestershire Record Office, catalogue D184.
2   *Victoria County History of Gloucestershire* (VCH), Vol. VIII, 1968, p. 8.
3   Readers are directed to N. Lloyd, *Gotherington Free Church 1833–1983* (Gotherington Free Church, 1983), for a full history of the church and its place in the history of the village.
4   GRO: P46 OV2/2.
5   Ibid.
6   GRO: P46 OV2/3.
7   Published as *Cheltenham Settlement Examinations*, ed. I. Gray (Bristol and Gloucestershire Archaeological Society, 1969).
8   Op. cit., p. 1.
9   Op. cit., p. 15.
10 Op. cit., pp. 68–9.
11 GRO: Q/Gc 5/5.
12 GRO: Q/Gc 5/4.
13 GRO: G/WI/95, *passim.*
14 GDR: Mary Jordan will, 1805.
15 Parish register held in Bishop's Cleeve church.
16 GRO: Q/Rel/1.
17 GRO: D2080 Vol. 8.
18 GRO: D2080 Vol. 583.
19 GRO: P46 OV8/37. Copies of the 1851 census returns are held in Gloucester Library.
20 VCH, p. 9.
21 Gloucester Library.
22 VCH, p. 7.
23 For a detailed history of the school, see O. Stinchcombe, *Lucky to Survive; a Centenary History of Gotherington School* (Chameleon Press, 1982).
24 Taken from VCH, Vol. II, p. 178.
25 A good collection of Kelly's Directories can be found in Gloucester Library.
26 Many details of the estate in the nineteenth century have been taken from the sale catalogues: GRO: SL64, SL484, upon which the next passage is based.

CHAPTER EIGHT

The Decline of the Old Order and the Beginning of the New

Gotherington 1894–1960

Geoffrey Pitt

'An eminently rural place is Gotherington, with its several considerable farm-houses and farm-yards, orchards and fowl-runs and old thatched or tile-roofed dwellings of shepherds and ploughmen and keepers of hens and bees. There are orchards on all sides and running chicken and waddling ducks everywhere, and cottages with outhouses and stores of fire-wood, with flower-beset paths leading to the doors. . . .' So wrote Dr Garrett in his book *From a Cotswold Height* in 1919, presenting a rather idealized picture which ignores the poor standard of the working-class cottages and the primitive sanitary arrangements that must have been obvious to him as he was the Medical Officer of Health for Cheltenham.[1] As previous chapters have shown, Gotherington had never been blessed with a resident lord of the manor who might have invested and provided leadership in mitigating the effects of the declining profitability of farming. For all the efforts of the estate agents in 1894 to encourage purchasers of the farms in the manor estate with stories that 'There is some capital society in the immediate area . . . the Cotswold and North Cotswold foxhounds and the Boddington harriers hunt the district and their meets give at least five days hunting a week. . . . Thriving woodland with a thick undergrowth capable of holding a good head of pheasants . . . Capital rough shooting on higher ground . . .' the farms were not an attractive proposition for those with ambitions to enjoy country life.[2] Matters were not to improve in the early years of the new century and the village had to suffer a long period of stagnation, one sign of which was that virtually no new houses were built. However, although this was clearly not a time of material prosperity, the years about the turn of the century saw a number of beneficial innovations in the village.

THE VILLAGE SCHOOL

As was explained in the previous chapter, Gotherington Board School was opened in 1881. Compared with those in the great majority of Gloucestershire villages, the school here was late in being founded because of local apathy, and its early years were indeed a struggle to survive.

The story of the school has been well told by Owen Stinchcombe in *Lucky to Survive*, but an interesting sidelight on events at this time is provided by a book of stories called *Methodist Idylls* published in 1897 under the name of Harry Lindsay.[3] The stories centre on a community called Woodleigh; the story-teller being the village schoolmaster. Woodleigh was

The view from the chapel down Cleeve Road, with the forge on the right and the school just to the left of the cottages on the left. There is little doubt Henry Lindsay was writing about Gotherington in *Methodist Idylls* in 1897. This photograph dates from about that time

said to be six miles from Spaton, with the chapel looking across the street at the forge on one side and the school on the other. The identification of the fictional Woodleigh with Gotherington is strengthened by the fact that the first master of the Board School here was called Henry Lindsay Hudson. Most of the stories in the book are examples of Victorian fiction in the typical highly moral, nonconformist pattern, but one tells of the arrival in the village of Arthur Rosson, a newly qualified teacher, and the scandalous attempts by the majority of the School Board to prevent him from educating the children 'to sich a pitch that 'em ud be no good for work' (as farm labourers, of course), and to avoid all unnecessary expense to the ratepayers.

While some of the characters are fictional, the chief villain of the story bears the same name as a man who lived in the village at the time and it is hard to avoid the conclusion that this story is thinly disguised autobiography and a form of revenge from afar for Henry Hudson who had found life under the School Board unbearable and had resigned his post after one year. From a distance of a hundred years the rights and wrongs of the case cannot be established and are of less interest than the impression given of a community becoming more polarized, part wanting to move with the times and part wanting to maintain the status quo, or at least afraid to offend their masters. Those who are impatient for change have a hard task to overcome the reaction of the established farming community and often give up and move away like Henry Hudson. At all times in its history, Gotherington experienced the tensions between the new and the old. Our story is the poorer in having to wait until almost our own day before we can learn about the human response to these tensions.

Continuing lack of support for the school led to a succession of early resignations (there were ten headteachers in the first thirty-two years), and it was only with the arrival of Miss Sheaf in 1918 that the school had a headteacher with the vision and the determination to achieve the potential of the school in the face of the financial stringency of the time. This was

Gotherington School pupils, *c.* 1904. Rural poverty can be seen in the hand-me-down clothes and lack of older pupils who had left school for work

made worse by the lack of forcefulness on the part of the managers in pressing the county education committee for improvements to a very inferior set of buildings, and by declining numbers of pupils – down from about a hundred in the 1880s to forty-six in 1918 – which threatened the continued existence of the school.

Miss Sheaf had the advantage of arriving at a time when education methods were undergoing changes for the better, and she made full use of the opportunities, encouraging the more able children to work for scholarship places at grammar schools (and to set their sights on better jobs than farm labouring) with remarkable success considering the small numbers in the school. Her twenty-five years at the school are remembered not only as a time of achievement in academic terms but also as a happy time for the pupils. Until 1929 the school catered for children throughout their entire school life but thereafter those of eleven years and over were sent to the senior school at Bishop's Cleeve or, if they passed the scholarship examination, to the grammar school in Cheltenham. Those who went to Cheltenham were something of a race apart in their schools as 'train children' whose arrival and departure were governed by the timetable of the railway, not that of the school. The change in 1929 reduced the number of pupils at Gotherington to thirty but, although the numbers remained small and the standard of the premises poor, the school served the village well.

CHURCH AND CHAPEL

In Chapter 5 it was related that Gotherington came near to becoming a separate parish from Bishop's Cleeve during the seventeenth-century Commonwealth period, but churchgoers still had to go to Cleeve until the 1920s when a church-room was opened for some services in the

Ivyville played an important part in the lives of Gotherington people in the nineteenth and early twentieth centuries. It was at different times the post office, reading room and Anglican place of worship

front room of Ivyville. Soon afterwards, in 1933, Gotherington was transferred from Bishop's Cleeve parish to Woolstone and Oxenton which meant that it ceased to represent about one-quarter of the parishioners of a very large parish and became the largest numerical part of a smaller parish. Changes are never universally acceptable and some Gotherington people continued (and continue even now) to attend services in Bishop's Cleeve, but most came to terms with it, perhaps encouraged at the time by the rector's wisdom in continuing to hold some services in the village, latterly in the village hall.

The history of the Free church has been ably written by Reverend Norman Lloyd who made a thorough study of the many surviving records for his book, *Gotherington Free Church 1833–1983*. At the start of this period the church had for twenty years relied on St Andrew's Presbyterian church in Cheltenham for supervision and the provision of preachers but there was a growing sense of independence which culminated in their taking full control of their affairs in 1909. Although the original trust deed of 1846 shows that the church formed part of the Countess of Huntingdon's Connexion from its foundation in 1833, the association remained less than a formal affiliation until as late as the 1960s, the property finally being conveyed to the trustees of the Connexion after about twenty years of hesitation. As with most rural chapels, it survived and played an important role in the life of the village through the exertions of a dedicated band of local people and the support given by lay preachers who came out from Cheltenham to take the services.

EARNING A LIVING

In the 1891 census twenty-two Gotherington men described themselves as farmers, working the land with the help of sixteen farmers' sons and fifty-eight labourers, which indicates an average farm size of about sixty acres.[4] On small unimproved farms such as these, farmers were not prospering and their labourers were faring very badly. In the decade to 1910, average labourers' wages were 10*s* to 12*s* 6*d* per week with perhaps a few potatoes extra, while food

The Shutter Inn was at least 150 years old when photographed here in 1925

prices were increasing faster than wages and there was always the prospect of being laid off work without pay in bad weather. Farmers and farm labourers represented 70 per cent of the men in the village aged between fifteen and sixty-five in 1891. Gotherington was still the farming community of its past but as time went on fewer labourers were needed because farmers turned more and more from arable to livestock raising. Between 1874 and 1938 the area under the plough in Gloucestershire decreased by nearly two thirds and the number of cattle increased by nearly a half.[5]

Another 9 per cent of the men of working age in 1891 were the village craftsmen – blacksmiths, carpenters and wheelwrights, shoemakers and stonemasons – with which this village had always been well endowed. They too found their services less and less in demand as fewer ploughs, harrows and scythes were used and, later, the horse and cart began to be replaced by motorized transport, while shoes could be produced more cheaply in large factories elsewhere and bricks could be economically produced and transported by rail to compete with the local building stone. The period between 1894 and 1960 not only saw the decline of the farming community, but also its craftsmen. In the 1950s one carpenter was still at work in a small way, principally as a coffin-maker for local people, but it was the baker who was the last tradesman to remain in business, as late as the 1980s, longer after the others had gone. The Shutter Inn (and the associated Malt Shovel) and the Farmers' Arms, which had previously provided work locally for maltsters and brewers, no longer did so after 1892 when the Shutter Inn was bought by the Cheltenham Original Brewery and the Farmers' Arms was bought by a Cheltenham builder and leased to Flowers.[6]

Other ways of making a living were adopted. Most of the cottages had gardens and some had small orchards, and a number of people made use of their land to grow produce which they took to Cheltenham to sell – often on foot and, in at least one case, twice a day during the strawberry season. The change from farm labouring to market gardening was an attractive way of eliminating the dependence on the farmer, but the gardener was left with the additional task of finding purchasers for his produce.

Over the years, the possibility of making a living from a shop in the village had been

The Farmers' Arms was built by John Perry in 1833

recognized from at least as early as 1841, and quite a number can be identified from directories in the later years of the nineteenth century onwards. They functioned in one room of a house or cottage, offering for sale any groceries or household requirements which villagers were prepared to buy, but most of these enterprises had limited lives for one reason or another and generally provided work for no one outside the owner's family. Butchers set up in business in 1906 and bakers in 1914. A post office opened in Rowanside, Malleson Road in 1894 with a telegraph service added in 1897, the office migrating successively to Ivyville, the Laurels and Woolstone View in Malleson Road during this period before finding a home in Ryman's village shop.[7] A public telephone was installed in the post office in Ivyville in the 1920s and subsequently replaced by a call box on the opposite side of the road, where it remained for many years until being moved to its present position by the old school playground. Facilities were thus becoming more available in the village, supplemented by travelling salesmen such as Giles and Lusty who called with hardware, kindling, paraffin and other household goods on a weekly round of local villages from about the turn of the century (Giles & Co. are still trading in the district). A photographer from Alderton toured the area on foot and some of his prints are among the earliest visual records of the community. It is not surprising in view of the reduced job prospects that the population which had reached a peak of 424 in 1851, had fallen to 364 in 1891 and remained at about 340 up to 1951, whereas the population of England increased by over 60 per cent between 1851 and 1891, and by 50 per cent again between 1891 and 1951. The drift away to the towns (and the colonies) was similar to that in many rural areas, consisting mainly of men and women in the younger age groups who would normally have been the mainstay in keeping the village alive and growing.

It is rarely possible to discover where people went, although Cheltenham must have been a powerful magnet with many houses requiring domestic servants. Some went much further. Isaac Peart, from the family of masons, emigrated to Australia in 1884 at the age of twenty-one, found work within two months, was farming on his own account in 1890 and had 4,000 acres by 1906. Another emigrant to Australia was less fortunate, losing his life and leaving a widow with four young children to be brought home to Gotherington by her father, Edward Holbrook. The 1891 census records two more people returned from abroad: one was a nine year old girl born in Bombay and apparently sent home by her grandparents to go to school. The other was a woman of forty born 'on seagoing to India'. Of the 362 people in Gotherington in 1891, 155 were born elsewhere in Gloucestershire (including Woolstone, Oxenton and Bishop's Cleeve), thirty-six came from other parts of England and Wales and three from abroad; more than half were not born in Gotherington.

In the First World War most of the young men joined the armed forces, leaving the older men to keep the farms going. Before the outbreak of the war, this country had imported three-quarters of its wheat, half its meat, three-quarters of its cheese and seven eighths of its butter consumption, so the shipping losses resulting from the U-boat campaign caused national concern over food shortages. Between 1914 and 1915 food prices increased by 30 per cent and then by 60 per cent by the next year, following a harvest of small volume and poor quality. Effective action was eventually taken: prices were controlled, executive committees were set up and instructed farmers what crops were to be grown and what additional land had to be cultivated. With price support, advice and encouragement an increase in output was achieved but soon after the war ended the government allowed the guaranteed price system to lapse and farming returned to its previous inefficient, unprofitable ways, unable to compete with imported food. The farm labourer's wage which had risen to £3 per week during the war soon fell by a half. By this time, ten of the young men from the village were dead, at least one was incapacitated and many of the others had seen enough of the world to realize that there were better jobs than farming, though the prospects remained poor throughout the 1920s.

IMPROVING THE VILLAGERS – THE IMPACT OF THE MALLESONS

Many small villages around the country went through similarly depressing times during this period but few of them can have benefited from the sort of lucky chance which led Frank and Elizabeth Malleson to take up residence in Dixton Manor when they retired from London some twelve years before this period starts.[8] They were to contribute two more innovations for the benefit of Gotherington. For many years previously they had shown a remarkable talent and energy for providing educational and welfare facilities for working people in the capital, and their activities were to continue here even though their move to Gloucestershire was made because of indifferent health. As they travelled about from their new home they had the opportunity to observe and reflect on the hardship of the farm labourer's life and to debate together what might be done to improve his lot.

They were concerned first of all that no trained nursing help was available in rural areas, with the result that childbirth and emergencies could easily lead to fatal consequences by the time someone could be found to go to Winchcombe and summon the doctor. At one time he would come attired in a tall hat adorned with a cockade, riding in a gig driven by a coachman. Mrs Malleson was a very persuasive campaigner and fund-raiser and, although she was met with indifference by many of the better-off members of Gloucestershire society, she won sufficient support to have a nurse-midwife trained and installed in a cottage in Aggs Lane on a trial basis in 1885 and on a more permanent basis in 1889. The nurse had a hard life with sixteen villages or hamlets to serve in a radius of four miles, travelling in a governess cart pulled by a donkey in all weathers in return for a pound per week plus accommodation, board and uniform. Most of those who took the job on did not stay for long but the experiment was undoubtedly a success and of great value to people in the area. Thanks to Mrs Malleson, Gotherington was in at the foundation of the Rural Nursing Association, the forerunner of the district nursing concept, in marked contrast to the tardy establishment of the Board School for which the village had no enthusiastic persuader to energize them.

The Mallesons also noted that the typical farm labourer's cottage provided only a general purpose living-room for the whole family so that the labourer returned from a long day's work in winter with the prospect of spending an evening in the only room with a fire, surrounded by a noisy bunch of youngsters and all the household activities in progress. By their middle-class standards the labourer deserved conditions more conducive to relaxation and recuperation (while his wife coped with the children and the chores, naturally). The village pub was not the answer in their view because it would have rapidly siphoned off the week's wages; instead they instituted a Reading Room and Village Club in two rooms rented from Mrs Willis in Ivyville in 1885. Here the men and boys over fourteen could meet during the winter evenings, play cards, bagatelle, draughts and dominoes, read the newspapers provided, exchange library books and attend talks and courses, all for a nominal subscription of a penny per week. Women were catered for during two afternoons a week when they were encouraged to read the newspapers and attend classes in reading, knitting and cookery.[9]

The new lord of the manor, another absentee like all those before him, distanced himself from the enterprise on the grounds that it would be impossible to keep the club non-political; the Mallesons were Liberals and Mr Hutchinson a Tory, of course. He also feared that if he supported it and it failed he would be called upon to pay its debts. (He lived in Rosehill at the corner of New Barn Lane and the Evesham Road, now demolished and replaced by Gulf Oil's headquarters. His income from Gotherington Manor estate alone was over £900 per annum.)[10] However, the venture was a success, the membership was about thirty and when problems were encountered over the renewal of the lease in 1903 they were quickly overcome by the building of a new Reading Room, the front portion of the present Village Hall. Frank Malleson died in that year but his widow and their daughters continued to provide the vision, drive and (inevitably) some financial support which ensured that the club made a valuable contribution to the life of the village. After Mrs Malleson died in 1916 the range of activities offered decreased gradually and at the same time the growing availability of radio and cheaper newspapers reduced the usefulness of the club, the membership declining to about ten in the

The Reading Room before the rear extension was added in 1962

mid-1930s and eventually to zero. The building, however, continued to provide a most useful centre for social events and, after the Second World War, for a baby clinic, meetings of a branch of the Women's Institute and an increasing range of social and recreational activities. Once again, the advantage of having an outside catalyst is apparent, for it seems likely that without the Mallesons the village would not have had a hall until much later.

THE PARISH COUNCIL

An important development in local government occurred at the beginning of this period with the inauguration of parish councils in 1894. Elections had to be held and three Gotherington farmers, one of the local blacksmiths and the innkeeper of the Farmers' Arms took up their duties as councillors at the first meeting on 19 December of that year, with a treasurer from the Capital and Counties Bank in Cheltenham and the clerk, H.W. Stephens, a solicitor from Cheltenham, presumably appointed or at least recommended by Winchcombe Rural District Council. (This was the body at that time responsible for the local government of Gotherington). Mr Stephens would have been a source of guidance (for five pounds a year, but soon reduced to three) at a time when the councillors were inevitably without experience of any such office.[11] However, the fact that he happened to be the clerk to the RDC raises some question concerning the wisdom of the choice!

In the early years of the parish council there were frequent changes of councillors so that twenty-two served in the first twenty years; only two provided real continuity, Sam Price and William Reeves, who served for forty-five and twenty-seven years respectively. The minutes of the first few quarterly meetings suggest that there was little or no business to transact but the council soon began to find its feet and play an increasing role especially in referring complaints to Winchcombe over such matters as the excessively high rating valuation of the parish, the absence of a proper water supply and the muddy state of the footpath used by Gotherington people walking across the fields to the parish church in Bishop's Cleeve. Some topics were still on the agenda over forty years later, including nuisance from the parish drain in Woolstone Lane, first raised in 1909 but an echo from the Middle Ages, and the illegal use of the footpath by the Malt Shovel by cyclists and horse riders (1911).

From time to time the council minutes help the present-day reader to appreciate better what life was like in those days; for instance, they record a deliberation on the question of whether to pay a subscription towards the manual fire-engine operated by a team of volunteers in Bishop's Cleeve. At a later date, a steam-powered engine could be summoned from Cheltenham and, on one occasion, it was reported to have reached the fire in forty minutes from receiving the call (1906). A more contemporary note is struck in 1932 when the proposal to transfer the administration of the parish from Winchcombe RDC to Cheltenham RDC predictably led to protests.

The RDC seems to have been tardy if not deliberately uncooperative over some of the matters raised. In 1906 a dispute arose over the responsibility for the repair of a road surface in Granna Lane which was (correctly but with dubious relevance) described as the only road connecting the trams on Cleeve Hill with Gotherington station. This led to the parish council making a complaint against the RDC to the County Council and the holding of a public hearing in the Reading Room, at which the parish's case had to be presented by another Cheltenham solicitor because H.W. Stephens was presenting Winchcombe's case. The parish council won the day but the RDC evaded full compliance with the ruling, saying that the stone dressing which had eventually been supplied could not be rolled in by steam-roller because of the risk of damaging the drain at the bottom of the lane; the lumps were said to be the size of two fists. The local press reported the hearing in some detail with a picture of the parish councillors standing resolute across the road outside the Reading Room.[12]

The Parish Council and the RDC did not hold one another in the highest of esteem.

When the parish raised another matter a year later, the following exchange occurred in the RDC meeting:

Mr Preston: 'That has been done a long time ago. I wish the council had got something else to do.'

Mr Groves: 'Tell them to get about in the daylight, not grope about at night.'

The muddy state of the coffin path to Bishop's Cleeve church and the smell of the parish drain are the sort of matters which made daily life more unpleasant than need be in the village and the council performed a useful task in urging action to rectify them even though little was sometimes achieved. Potentially more serious problems were presented by the arrival of seven or eight hundred navvies engaged on the construction of the railway line from Honeybourne through Winchcombe to Bishop's Cleeve and Cheltenham. For some time they lived in huts in the field opposite The Folly in cramped, insanitary conditions that made the risk of contagion very high. A case of smallpox in a hut where twenty-six men slept caused serious concern to the health authority particularly when it was discovered that twenty-one of the contacts had disobeyed instructions and vanished. The village school could not accommodate all the children from the navvies' families, a problem for which the education authority after much deliberation produced the solution of removing Woolstone children from Gotherington School to Oxenton School, to the dissatisfaction of everyone ('Parishes at variance', reported the *Cheltenham Free Press*). It will come as no surprise that by the time alternative arrangements were made the navvies had finished the local stretch of line and had moved on.[13]

NEW TRANSPORT LINKS

The Honeybourne to Cheltenham line was constructed by the Great Western Railway in an endeavour to prevent the rival Midland Railway from monopolizing traffic between Bristol and Birmingham, and it was completed in 1906 having cost half a million pounds.[14] Small

Gotherington station shortly after opening in 1906

country stations were sited to serve a number of villages and the position of Gotherington station was chosen with an eye to potential passengers from Dixton, Prescott and Woolstone, though some people from Gotherington must have found it more convenient to use Bishop's Cleeve station. Long-distance trains did not stop at the local stations but there were seven local trains each way in 1910 and ten in 1932 which were used by most of those employed or at school in Cheltenham. The alternative, Bowles bus service, passed infrequently along the Evesham Road but unlike the railway, could not transport prams and did not accept free travel permits issued to scholarship children. Some living at the west end of the village rode to school on bicycles supplied as an alternative to train passes.

The opening of the railway line was heralded in the *Cheltenham Free Press* with the expectation that Gotherington would prosper from the facilities afforded but it is clear that this did not occur to any great extent. Unlike the station at Toddington, which became a busy centre for the dispatch of fruit to distant markets, that at Gotherington appears to have been used mainly for sending milk and small consignments of local produce to Cheltenham and Gloucester. A few local men found work on the railway as station staff or maintenance men, the coal merchants in business at the station and opposite the forge would have obtained their supplies by rail but the other local enterprises started between the wars (tea-rooms, a garage and motorist's accommodation on the Evesham Road) had no connection with the railway and, in fact, were harbingers of the era of motor cars. By 1941 there was too little freight traffic to justify keeping the goods yard open and too few passengers to warrant the employment of staff here. The station was down-graded to an unmanned halt.

The attraction of a home in the country is believed to have brought a number of people who were not in business in Gotherington to occupy The Folly, Merecombes, Lilley Bank and Moat House, for example, at times between 1906 and 1939. It is possible that the first three properties were popular because the station was near at hand, and one man who lived at The Folly is known to have travelled to Birmingham to manage a business while others commuted to Cheltenham. None of these people, however, remained as long as seven years apparently. At about this time, Woodmancote and Cleeve Hill were attracting considerable

Mrs Lord's tea rooms on the Evesham Road

numbers of outsiders, the population growing from 310 to 1891 to 656 in 1931 and 1090 in 1951 in marked contrast to the absence of growth in Gotherington.[15]

By the 1950s the local railway service was losing the battle for passengers to the buses as in many other places. In 1955 five weekday trains would stop at Gotherington halt if requested, but by 1959 there were none even though the other stations on the line continued to operate.[16] In the following March all passenger services were withdrawn. By then, Kearsey buses made fifteen journeys between Gotherington village and Cheltenham on weekdays while Bristol Omnibus Company services from Cheltenham to Tewkesbury and Evesham made fifteen and twelve journeys respectively, stopping at Gotherington crossroads. Not only were the bus services more frequent but they had the advantage of picking up and setting down passengers at more convenient points than the railway, and charged lower fares because they were not saddled with the cost of permanent way maintenance.

HOW POOR WERE THE VILLAGERS?

When Miss Sheaf came to the village in 1918 she was shocked to discover a family of eight children with only two pairs of shoes between them who therefore had to attend school in rotation. While this was clearly an example of real poverty in the village, it would seem to have been an extreme case to imprint itself in her memory, to be recalled many years later. It is difficult to assess the degree of poverty which existed in those days since the standard of living today is so much higher even than that enjoyed by better-off people sixty or seventy years ago. Working-class houses varied from the very old thatched cottage with leaky roof and rotting timbers, coming to the end of its days, to the small but more serviceable brick-built nineteenth-century cottage with a slate roof and stone floor which was still cold and damp in winter. Farmers who owned cottages for their workers spent little on their upkeep. Some homes had a piped water supply from the private reservoir at Manor Farm for which a water

The photograph of the interior of Gotherington School referred to in the text

rate was payable, but many were dependent on wells or pumps. Earth closets with euphemistic names such as Rose Cottage or The Houses of Parliament were commonly situated at the end of the garden.

Household furniture and possessions were simple and often handed down from a previous generation. Clothes were strong, hardwearing and painstakingly repaired for ordinary use while a few special items were carefully stored to wear on occasions. In so far as can be judged from photographs which survive from the inter-war years it does not seem that there was really dire poverty in the village such as had occurred in the previous century and or was still occurring in urban slum areas, though no one would pretend that people were well off. Jobs were lost here as everywhere else in the depression, and the dole (unemployment benefit) was of limited value and was only extended to agricultural workers in 1936. Admittedly most of the photographs are of special occasions and they may not present a fair cross-section of the community. A photograph of a school class in about 1930 can perhaps be accepted as evidence that at that time the children look adequately fed and clothed, much more so than children in the poorer districts of industrial towns. (Moreover, the class-room was furnished with tables and arm-chairs whereas most schools then still used old-fashioned straight-backed desks.) There was undoubtedly a good deal of mutual help: clothes would be handed on to be remade for the next user, friends and neighbours would share in the bounty when a pig was killed, the old and infirm were cared for and the large family whose small cottage was at bursting point were able to board out a child with a neighbour who had a spare bed. Working-class expectations were few but at least the institution of the old age pension shortly before the First World War caused the spectre of the workhouse to recede.[17]

Marion Holmes in her book *A Patchwork Quilt* gave her recollections of growing up in the inter-war years in a family which had members who were small farmers and gardeners.[18] Here mutual help extended in both directions: the family benefited from the receipt of generous

WON 14 DRAWN 1. Cheltenham League Div. 3. 1927-8
GOTHERINGTON A.F.C. 1928.

Football has been a popular recreational activity in many local villages throughout the twentieth century, and Gotherington is no exception; this is the team of 1928

Christmas hampers from a benefactor in the West Country, while they gave a home to a tragically widowed aunt left without means of support, and presented gifts to a widow with an epileptic son in the village. As she records, entertainment was mostly organized in the community, the Reading Room and the school hall providing meeting places. This was the heyday of 'home-made' entertainment, dancing to music played by the local jazz band, comic cricket matches (in drag), whist drives as well as the church fête and the celebration of May Day and Empire Day at the school. There were local league football matches behind Hales Farm. A visit to Denley's Eversfield Pleasure Garden at Bishop's Cleeve was a real source of excitement for the children, as was a trip to the Mop Fair at Tewkesbury. The Mallesons once again acted as unofficial benevolent squires by providing Christmas parties for the schoolchildren at Dixton Manor.

A number of families were able to benefit from the opportunity to supplement their income by growing some food on allotments set up in 1920 under a national scheme. The parish council secured a lease on the first field to the west of 93 Malleson Road, large enough to provide fourteen quarter-acre, three half-acre and four one-acre plots. One of the local farmers and two market gardeners jumped at the chance of an extra acre of land and there appears to have been no difficulty in finding takers for the other eighteen plots. The original rent is not known but after the derating of land it fell to £3 12s per acre in 1929 and £3 3s in 1935.[19] The Parish Council managed the scheme, upbraiding tenants who failed to keep their plots in order and dealing discreetly with the occasional unforeseen problem:

December 1935: 'Allotment hedges to be trimmed by parish council when condition warrants it.'

March 1936: 'Chairman had received complaints of difficulties arising from cutting low of the allotment hedges. Resolved that a latrine of iron or iron and wood be erected at the lower end of the allotments.'

The 1920 allotment scheme was not as ambitious as a previous one set up as long ago as 1844 by a Captain Ruddle, a prosperous retired seafarer and overseas trader of Walton House and later The Mythe, Tewkesbury, on fifty acres of land he purchased at Gotherington Fields behind what is now Ruddles Farm (which he had built). At £4 10s per acre rent the venture would have yielded him 8 per cent on the purchase price, less expenses, a good return for those days. Seventy tenants were attracted from Gotherington, Woolstone, Bishop's Cleeve, Woodmancote, Ashchurch and Brockhampton even though some would have had a long walk before and after the evening's work. Forty-four tenants were from Gotherington and they were mostly farm labourers though some of the local farmers again took on one-acre plots. The scheme ran for at least thirty-five years and there is some evidence to suggest that it may have continued until the First World War, though later references may have been to allotments on land behind Gorse Green about 1900.[20] The nineteenth-century rules were strict but of practical value:

No work on the Sabbath
Not to injure neighbour's crops, nor trespass
Not more than half of plot to be sown with the same sort of crop in any year
Not more than two-thirds of the summer crop to be harvested until the September rent is paid
No flax, hemp or rape to be grown

The 1920 allotment field was less than one fifth as big but more conveniently situated for Gotherington people. This scheme continued to operate until 1962 when a new lease would have raised rents to a level which tenants were not prepared to pay.

The 1930s saw a gradual small measure of improvement in the general standard of living thanks to the availability of some more jobs in Cheltenham, and cheaper food prices; imports of Argentine beef, Danish bacon and wheat at glut prices helped the housewife but not the British farmer who gathered in the smallest harvest on record in 1931. The farm labourer still had a raw deal. At least two local farmers were prosecuted in the 1930s for not paying the minimum wage to their employees. One man was paid £1 7s instead of £1 14s 6d in summer and £1 16s in winter and was not paid for overtime, nor was he given any half-days off; the farmer was fined £5 and ordered to pay £44 arrears.[21] In another case where no payment was made for work on Saturday afternoon or Sunday, the farmer's solicitor explained in court that the man had been allowed time off whenever he wanted it and had been given a very generous ration of cider every day; the farmer was fined £2 and ordered to pay £11 arrears. The press report described the fines as heavy.[22]

Another improvement to life in the village in the 1930s was the provision of some mains services: coal gas from Cheltenham gas-works and mains electricity both arrived during this decade but mains water did not reach all the houses until about 1942 and mains sewage was not installed until 1959.[23]

THE SECOND WORLD WAR AND AFTER

National concern over food supplies again developed early in the Second World War and controls were re-imposed on farming activities. The first tractor in the village, purchased by a local farmer, appeared in 1940 and, among other machinery, a grain drier supplied by the War Agricultural Committee was later put to good use. Much of the surrounding farm land is heavy clay and its cultivation was made much easier by the use of a tractor as compared with horses. There were other changes as in most rural areas: children were brought here as

The Second World War ammunition dump in Gotherington Fields disappeared during the writing of this book. Eric Reynolds' drawing captures the atmosphere better than any photograph

107

evacuees from London, Guernsey and Bristol (one married a Gotherington lady about fifty years later), members of the Women's Land Army worked on farms in the area (two married local farmers rather more quickly), women from the village helped to swell the ranks of workers on Smiths' assembly lines while Italian, German, Polish and Ukrainian prisoners were housed at Sudeley and worked on public works and on the farms. The US Army set up a depot in a field alongside Gotherington Lane beyond the present-day Homelands Farm, one of many in this country where equipment was assembled for dispatch to the second front. Gotherington Fields Farm was taken over by the Ministry of Agriculture, and at the far end of the lane under the trees by the present-day boarding kennels there was an ammunition dump in Nissen huts, the last vestiges of which can still be seen. The war was brought right into the village when the *Luftwaffe* dropped bombs across the western side one night, severely damaging a house in Longfurlong and destroying a thatched cottage in Shutter Lane, killing the occupant, Miss Kearsey.[24] One local man serving in the RAF lost his life.

The minutes of the Parish Council give little indication that there was a war on, concentrating on local concerns such as the mounds of clay left around after the installation of water pipes demanding attention, justifiably no doubt because of the potential hazard in the black-out. When the hostilities ceased, the council discussed the form that victory celebrations should take and the minutes record that Mr Cook had offered a sheep subject to the consent of the Food Executive Officer. As with many items in the minutes, there is no indication of the outcome but it would be hard to imagine the request being refused at such a time.

Food rationing and other wartime restrictions were to continue in the 1950s and were only gradually removed. Very little building work was permitted. No. 93 Malleson Road was built in 1946 on what was then a small holding, while No. 91 (thatched at the time) was saved from the threat of demolition by the council as an unfit dwelling, by the installation of bathroom, cloakroom, larder and hot-water system.[25] Six semi-detached Airey houses were built by Cheltenham Rural District Council in 1947 in Woolstone Lane and a brick-built pair was added at the junction with Malleson Road in 1952.[26] Planning permission for new houses began to be granted but normally only on infilling sites which had been old orchards now deemed of no importance between existing houses. Developers made careful study of the old editions of the Ordnance Survey 1:2500 maps for suitable sites and were well rewarded in Gotherington. In the middle of the 1950s the building of groups of houses such as 61 to 67 Malleson Road was in progress and, at the end of the decade, 6 to 14 Gretton Road. The new houses were occupied predominantly by people from elsewhere, including those coming to take up work at GCHQ, Smiths' Industries, the Coal Research Establishment and Dowtys. For the first time, the ten-year census was to show a marked increase from 341 in 1951 to 457 in 1961.

In the early 1950s the influx was on a relatively small scale and could be assimilated without much change to the nature of the village, which still looked like a village. Hales Farm, Moat Farm and Home Farm, for example, were still obviously farms surrounded by fields in which cattle would graze, poking their heads over the hedge at passers-by. Farm animals were frequently moved to and from the more distant fields on the hoof along the road, men went to the allotments with home-made cider to refresh them, the bar in the Shutter Inn had sawdust on the floor and at ten o'clock the door was closed to the sound of 'Goodnight Tom', 'Goodnight George' as the bicycles were mounted and then silence reigned.

The new arrivals inevitably brought their own ideas with regard to leisure activities and facilities, how their children should be taught and such matters. The degree of success they achieved in integrating into the community is an open question. One early innovation was the establishment of a branch of the Women's Institute in 1953 with members drawn from the villagers and the newcomers. As time progressed, there were more new arrivals and more joined the WI. In drawing up the programmes for meetings the committee may well have received more suggestions for topics from the newcomers and consequently the emphasis may have shifted in a direction which made the meetings of less interest to the villagers. It is a matter for speculation how the branch might have developed if the influx of outsiders had been smaller.

The seeds of change were undoubtedly sown in the 1950s and their germination and development form the subject of the last chapter.

The War memorial

References

1   J.H. Garrett, *From a Cotswold Height* (1919, reprinted by Alan Sutton Publishing, Gloucester, 1988).
2   GRO: DL1388 SL8/12.
3   H. Lindsay, *Methodist Idylls* (London, 1897).
4   Copies of 1891 census returns in Gloucester Library.
5   L. Dudley Stamp, *The Land of Britain, its Use and Misuse*. Third Edition (London, 1962), p. 101.
6   GRO: D4858 2/1/1; Stratford-on-Avon Record Office DR 227.
7   *Kelly's Directory of Gloucestershire*. Various editions.
8   This passage relies on the brief study of the Mallesons: O. Stinchcombe, *Elizabeth Malleson (1828–1916) Pioneer of Rural District Nursing* (published privately, 1989).
9   O. Stinchcombe, 'Gotherington Reading Room and Village Club'. *Local History Bulletin* No. 45 (Gloucestershire Rural Community Council, 1982).
10 GRO: D1388/12.
11 Gotherington Parish Council, Minutes of meetings, *passim* (held by Gotherington Parish Council).
12 *Cheltenham Examiner*, Reports of RDC and PC meetings, 28 July 1906–15 April 1908; Report of Official Inquiry, 11 December 1907.
13 *Cheltenham Free Press*. Extract from Winchcombe Medical Officer's annual report, 24 February 1906.
14 *Cheltenham Free Press*, 11 August 1906.
15 Census figures are taken from Kelly's Directories.
16 *Bradshaw's Railway Guide* (London and Manchester, 1955); *Smart's Timetable for Cheltenham Spa* (Gloucester, 1959).
17 P. Horn, *Rural Life in England in the First World War* (Dublin, 1984).
18 M.I. Holmes, *A Patchwork Quilt* (Gotherington, 1991).

19 Details of the allotments are taken from Gotherington Parish Council, minutes of meetings 1919–62.
20 GRO: D2256 E4; reminiscences of Harry Haines recorded by O. Stinchcombe.
21 Press cutting, unreferenced.
22 Press cutting, unreferenced.
23 Gotherington Parish Council, minutes of meetings July 1931, June 1937, November 1939.
24 *Gloucestershire Echo*, 20 November 1940; *Cheltenham Chronicle*, 30 November 1940.
25 Local information.
26 Local information.

CHAPTER NINE

The End of a Traditional Way of Life

Gotherington Since 1960

Graham Teale

THE APPEARANCE OF THE VILLAGE

Since the 1950s the trends which were transforming a rural agricultural community into a residential settlement for people working outside the village accelerated. Although Gotherington is still surrounded by its fields it is no longer the working village of the past. Over two thousand years of history have been ended in the last thirty or forty years.

One of the most obvious ways that this can be seen is in the nature of the buildings. Since 1960 not only have many new houses been constructed, but many older ones reflecting the agricultural past have been demolished and replaced with dwellings. This process started in the nineteenth century but then such new building as The Holt was exceptional; now it is the norm. We can catalogue a roll-call of change.

Since 1960 the following have been pulled down: Yew Tree Cottage and The Stocks, both in Cleeve Road opposite the Old Forge; and a small cottage known as Follets Cottage between The Holt and Rutley Villa. Laurel Cottage stood where the entrance to Cobblers Close is now. In 1990 the house next to Gotherington Cross Garage was pulled down and in its place a new garage showroom has been built to complement the existing garage developments. On the main Evesham Road two cottages have been pulled down, one at the end of Longfurlong Lane now replaced by the large red house. The other stood nearer the Farmers' Arms. Both cottages were red bricked. Malleson Road also has seen some cottages pulled down. The first cottage in from the Evesham Road was pulled down. On its ground now stands three new houses. This process was repeated further along, about fifty metres on the left before the Shutter Inn. Some old cottages have been renovated and greatly extended so that their old appearance has been changed, like Shady Nook in Shutter Lane, Cherry Furlong in Malleson Road, and Stoneville in Malleson Road where outbuildings have been converted into a dwelling house. In Manor Lane, Woods Cottage has been demolished and a new bungalow built on the site. The last cottage on Cleeve Road was known in earlier years as the Carpenters' Arms because Mr W. Wyman did carpentry work and made coffins in the old cottage, and of course made cider there. The next owner Mr Tom Long also made cider there, and many a barrel was consumed on the premises, hence the nickname Carpenters' Arms. Unlike many other cottages this has now been renovated. Since 1960 the number of houses has trebled. Brand new houses were built in Gretton Road in 1960/1, Manor Lane in 1962/3, The Lawns in 1961/4, Pullen Court in 1970, Cobblers Close in 1979, Ashmead Drive in 1963/4, Stonehouse Green in 1970 and Yew Tree Drive in 1969/70.

Gotherington in 1960; the view down Malleson Road

Gotherington in 1993; a longer view down Malleson Road. Rhondda Cottage in the distance was built during the eighteenth century to house the poor of Woolstone

Most of the houses in The Lawns were built between 1961 and 1964. Their newness and intrusiveness is well captured on this aerial photograph of the time (B. Shelmerdine)

The increasing number of houses and growing population led to further changes. Road widening took place in Malleson Road and Gretton Road in 1969 and some bends straightened, especially the right and left hander just by the Shutter Inn. It was a regular place in winter months for cars skidding off the road and ending up in Barefoot's Orchard. When the sewage system was installed in 1960 the roads had to be dug up and the contractors had problems with the pipe trenches filling with water; constant pumping was the order of the day through most of the village.

Village recreational amenities were also enlarged. The village hall, previously known as the Reading Room, was extended in 1962 with funds raised by the villagers and with the aid of the Department of Education and Science, and County Council grants. A store room was added in 1969. A small car park was also constructed in front of the hall and it is run by a committee made up of representatives of the parish council and local organizations.

Growing demand led to the playing field being acquired by the parish council in 1964. It comprises about four acres and was opened in 1965, paid for partly by grants, partly by subscription and partly by a loan repayable over sixty years. A rate levied on Gotherington householders for the playing field was to pay off the loan and contribute to its development and maintenance. The playing field is the property of the Gotherington Parish Council, and Gotherington has authority to levy rates but the villagers of Woolstone and Oxenton have equal access to the field and they contribute the equivalent of a 1p rate each year, which they raise by public subscription. In 1966 the Boys' Club building was erected on the playing field. It is run by a management committee of the entire parish council plus representatives of village organizations. Without the village hall and playing field, and the hard work of the committees getting these amenities into existence the village would be a poorer place. They are all symbols of increased leisure in the modern age – an aspect of life now taken for granted but so precious to villagers in earlier periods of history. Significantly much of the finance for many of the modern developments has come from outside the village.

These changes in Gotherington since 1960 have been emphasized by the decline in the working farm units in the village, in some cases ending a connection that can be traced to the twelfth century. Several farms in the village have disappeared since 1960. Yew Tree Farm in Cleeve Road, owned by W.J. Oldacre and used as a pig unit, was sold and houses built on the land, but the farmhouse is still there. Brick House Farm in Gretton Road had land sold off for building but again the farmhouse is still there; it is now called Dormer House. Baldwin's Farm in Gretton Road is no longer farmed; the farmhouse has been renovated and the barns converted. At Home Farm in Malleson Road the frontage has been sold off for building and the farmhouse is now used as a private dwelling. Back building has also occurred there. At Moat Farm in Malleson Road, built on the site of the medieval moated house of the Pendock family, the frontage has been sold off and the farmhouse is now used as private dwelling, with bed and breakfast, riding stables and cider manufacturers. Hales Farm in Malleson Road still has some fields which are let to nearby farmers. At Gotherington Fields Farm most of the land has been sold off to Mr M. Hocken of Woolstone from where it is still being farmed. So is Trumans Farm in Manor Lane, the last surviving agricultural unit around the manor-house at Upper Gotherington. Granna Farm in Gretton Road is no longer farmed but Greenway Farm in Granna Lane still exists as a smallholding with horticulture. White House Farm in the Evesham Road was farmed from 1957 and then a new farmhouse was built at the rear, called Orchard House Farm, in 1976. This was later sold and the farm continues from a bungalow, also built on the land.

The Shutter Inn has seen many alterations, and a complete renovation in recent years. Another building that has changed greatly since 1960 is Gotherington Cross Garage which has

The County Store at 15 Gretton Road was a shortlived venture as a village shop

vastly altered from the days of Mr Dickie Barrow when it was a black shed, an old-fashioned type of garage. Today it is a modern garage with showroom forecourt and repair shop at the rear. Just across the Evesham Road from the garage on the Cleeve side is the entrance to Longfurlong caravan site which was started in the early 1960s by the Robson family. It has changed hands and developed over the years to its present attractive site for mobile homes.

The years since 1960 have seen many changes in the traders in the village. Ryman's stores was first The Gables; their butchers shop has been and gone. Before they took over the post office it was at Woolstone View run by Mrs R. Edginton. Another general grocers was at 15 Gretton Road, but it has for twenty years been converted back to a bungalow. The bakehouse on Gretton Road had been in the Price family for three generations but it closed down in November 1990. However, Mavis Price's Hair Fashions continues on the same site as the bakery. A variety of traders have visited and continue to visit the village: milk is delivered, clothes laundered, hardware and fish can be bought.

We seem to be living in an age of ever-increasing change. Certainly many of the changes that have occurred since the 1960s have cut Gotherington off from its rural past. As this section has shown, such a fact is obvious to anyone who takes a walk around the village on any Sunday afternoon.

PEOPLE

In the 1950s of the few newcomers in the village many were working at the Coal Research Establishment in Stoke Orchard. Then as the village expanded the new occupants were working at either GCHQ, Smiths' Industries, Dowty Group Cheltenham and Ashchurch or the Central Electricity Generating Board. The people's occupations were now varied compared with the traditional village comprising farmers, farm labourers, traders and craftsmen. A common saying in the 1950s when someone was proposing a toast was 'Here's to a thousand a year' which never seemed likely (when wages were about £8 to £10 per week). Since 1960 the last of the great characters who had their roots in traditional village life have gone. They treasured their memories of the days before the modern changes and could remember well their childhood in an age of rural decline and comparative poverty in a village which changed its character as they grew up and grew old.

One exceptional person was Mr Charles Reginald Dawes who lived at Lillybank, the four hundred year old half-timbered cottage in Granna Lane. He spent the whole of his adult life building his collection of rare books; when he died thirty years ago at the age of eighty-four he left behind a collection of nine thousand volumes. No one could put an accurate price on the collection, but Mr Dawes' companion and secretary for eighteen years, Mr Anthony Gordon-Hill, estimated its value at £20,000 in the 1970s. The books presented a remarkable spectacle to the bibliophiles who travelled from all over the world to see them. The tightly packed shelves lined every wall from floor to ceiling.

The cottage itself held four thousand books, with another five thousand on display in an annex attached to the main building. Mr Dawes started work on his collection at the age of twelve, collecting magazines and similar publications, but at seventeen began collecting rare books. When he died, the collection had become so vast that it took the British Museum official sent to Gotherington four days to go through it and catalogue the books. One of the most important parts of the collection was the section of erotic literature, these included a very early edition of the now famous *Fanny Hill* by John Cleland, the only known copy signed by the first owner, and *My Secret Life*, one of the world's rarest books. There are only seven known copies written late in the nineteenth century by an unknown author. Many of the books were taken away to the British Museum.

Another of Gotherington's famous personalities was Miss Marion Holmes, a lady of many talents, literary, musical and horticultural. Marion gave up poetry at the age of twelve which

A portrait of Marion Holmes in early life. She became one of Gotherington's characters and her reminiscences published by the society after her death have added much to our knowledge of the recent social history of the village

left a gap of thirty years before the muse started again in the 1950s. From then on her trail of success led to victory in the nationally contested Cheltenham Open Poetry Competition. Marion's literary talent first surfaced when she was seven. For five years she wrote copiously. Then her mother sent one of her poems to a critic for the *British Weekly* newspaper – May Byron – who was well known and also notoriously severe. May Byron's response was not a private reply but a review in the newspaper of a fine young talent. Yet from that time on Miss Holmes' supply of words dried up and she devoted herself more and more to music, becoming a private piano tutor. That and her other parallel career in horticulture at Bishop's Cleeve Nursery, kept her too occupied to reach for her pen. During wartime she ran the Gotherington first aid post. Marion was also for over forty years organist at the Free church in Gotherington, and the Gotherington and Woolstone Church of England. For over thirty years she was Sunday school superintendent and local youth leader.

It was one of her church young people's groups which prodded her back towards writing poetry. One Christmas, girls insisted on singing a curiously metered folk tune, Marion wrote some words and they seemed to go down well. At the next harvest festival she wrote a poem for the church magazine and from there the work found its way to a literary magazine which reprinted it in its world-wide edition. Later she met Gabrielle Ward of Bishop's Cleeve, winner of the first Cheltenham Open Poetry Competition in 1971, and was persuaded to join the Cheltenham Poetry Group. Marion's poems were published in many magazines. Her success was crowned by her winning of the Wilfrid M. Appleby Trophy at the Cheltenham Open Poetry Competition. Her winning poem 'Resurrection' describes the life cycle of a dragon-fly in stately, regular metre and rhyme, allied to rich, flowing language.

Like the watercolour paintings which were a fruit of yet another of Marion's talents, her poems were mostly based on nature themes, the product of a lifetime in the countryside and a natural affinity with plants and animals. Her reminiscences were published after her death under the title *A Patchwork Quilt* which gives us a personal description of Gotherington life in the middle years of the twentieth century.

Marion lived just long enough to see the return to Gotherington of three special people – the Baird brothers who were among the evacuees who came to the village in 1940. The fiftieth anniversary celebration will pass into history as a very special village event for those who remember the wartime evacuees. At 8 p.m. on 15 June 1990 they laid a yellow and white cushion of flowers with hands of friendship incorporated in it on the war memorial exactly fifty years to the minute since as small boys they came to the village. On the Saturday they were entertained to a surprise reunion party in the village hall. On the Sunday they laid another colourful wreath at Woolstone morning church service at the memorial to the only serviceman from the village to lose his life in the last war, John Cresswell. They knew John, of course, as lads and went to school together. Fifty years on the village showed great changes, but the friendships had endured.

THE PARISH COUNCIL

Gotherington Parish Council had five members from its inception in 1894 until 1965 and then the County Council authorized an increase to seven in view of the growth in population. It was further increased to nine in 1970. Chairmen since 1960 have been Mr Ted South, Mr Gordon Pullen, Mr David Freeman, Mr Alan Keyte, Mr John Woolley and Mr John Poole, the latter who died tragically and suddenly during the writing of this book. The council meets in the village hall on the second Tuesday of each month. The parish had a representative on the Cheltenham Rural District Council until 1974. Now its representative is on the Tewkesbury Borough Council. The annual parish meeting is held in the village hall when representatives from such organizations as the Boys' Club, School Managers and Neighbourhood Watch give a résumé of their year's activities. One of the extra things the parish council has had to look after is the playing field and one thing they do not have to look after are the former allotments which have been given up now. The following is a report from the *Gloucestershire Echo* in 1980 on these two subjects, which shows how the parish council works on the village's behalf.

> The question about whether allotment plots should be provided was the subject of a discussion at a meeting of the Gotherington parish council. The chairman, Coun. David Freeman said that the council had a statutory duty to consider a written request presented by six or more electors, and that such a request had been received. With the assistance of Coun. Jack Harvey he had been able to persuade a local landowner to offer two acres of land for the sum of £2,000. The necessary money could be obtained either by an increase in the special parish rate for one year, amounting to approximately 2.3p in the £, or by the raising of a loan for which interest would be charged at the rate of 14 per cent for between 25 and 40 years, or 18.1/8 per cent for any period up to 25 years. He thought that two acres would provide 40 plots, or slightly less if a vehicle width access path were to be provided. At present-day values he did not think that an annual rent of anything up to £10 would be too much to expect people to pay. Coun. Robert Shelmerdine said that in his opinion the principle of providing a special amenity of this nature for the benefit of a maximum of 40 villagers, to be subsidized by the rest of the local ratepayers, was quite wrong, especially in these days when every effort ought to be made to contain rate-borne expedition. In any case, residents ought to be given an opportunity of airing their views by making the matter a special item for discussion at a parish meeting.
>
> After the view of a number of visitors had been sought, it was agreed that a proposal

to purchase land for the purpose of providing allotment plots be put to the annual parish meeting on March 19. The clerk, Mr R.G. Collett, offered to provide special notices of the meeting and it was agreed that these be delivered by members as far as possible to every house. (Despite the interest shown at the time, the allotments closed in 1987.)

The Chairman of the Playing Field Management Committee, Mr John Virgo, explained the difficulties which he had to face because the constitution of the committee had made it unmanageable. Under the present rules every single organized body in the parish, whether they used the field or not, were entitled to send a representative, and all the nine parish councillors were members. He pressed for membership to be restricted in future to representatives from only those bodies which actually made use of the playing field, such as the Boys' Club, the cricket club, the recreational club and the tennis club, plus a smaller number of parish councillors.

It was agreed that the parish council agree to their number of representatives being reduced to five, and that Mr Virgo's full recommendations be considered at the playing field annual meeting.

EDUCATION

The 1960s were years of change in the education of the children of Gotherington. The village of Gotherington was growing and so were the numbers of school-age children. Headmistress Miss McKearney and infant teacher Miss Tidmarsh had fifty-two pupils in January 1960. This had grown to sixty by December 1960 when the number of pupils was sufficient for the managers to ask for another full-time teacher. This was agreed by the Chief Education Officer. At a meeting on 5 December 1960 the Primary Education Sub-Committee recognized that an expansion to the school was now required and an early plan to close the school and send the children to Bishop's Cleeve was cancelled. Advice from the County Planning Officer was that the population of Gotherington was to increase from 480 to between 1,140 and 2,000. It was therefore decided to amend the development plan to include the building of a new school in the village capable of accommodating two hundred and eighty pupils. A three acre plot at Brick House Farm was earmarked for a new school. Some time later the dream of a new school was shattered when the county decision was to build only a nucleus and to retain the old school. July 1961 saw a terrapin classroom installed at the latter behind the main classroom for the third teacher Mrs Esp, but the school was still overcrowded and by May 1962 pupil numbers had risen to eighty-one.

May 1964 saw the retirement of Mrs Ida Edgington who had been school cook since November 1949, six months after the canteen opened. When she took over there had been thirty-six children to cater for, at the end there were eighty-seven. Her prowess is legendary. Although working to a tight budget she was able to afford better food by finding cheap local sources of fruit and vegetables, making jam and bottling fruit. Her *pièce de résistance* was the Christmas party, which she sometimes funded by organizing a whist drive, while villagers contributed produce. She made traditional Christmas puddings and for the party dressed up in a white chef's hat, painted on a black moustache and goose-stepped in with the Christmas pudding!

A second terrapin was installed at the front of the school, where the old shed stood, in September 1964, and a fourth teacher, Mrs Thomas, was appointed. In March 1965, staff was increased by a part-time post for physical education and swimming instruction. This was filled by Mrs Price. In September 1965 children who left Gotherington School were no longer divided into those who went to the grammar schools in Cheltenham and Tewkesbury or the secondary modern school in Bishop's Cleeve, for Cleeve Comprehensive School was established for children of all abilities.

The acquiring of the Brick House Farm site had run into problems and a site at the western end of Malleson Road was a possibility but the original site was preferred. This was

The present Gotherington School

finally acquired in September 1966 by a Compulsory Purchase Order. Plans for three classrooms and a kitchen were approved but, due to the re-routing of footpaths, building did not start until October 1967. The official opening ceremony was performed by Mr P. Milroy, Chief Education Officer for Gloucestershire, who unveiled a bronze plaque inscribed 'Gotherington Primary School opened 12th July 1968'. The school like the village continued to expand. In January 1970 a fifth full-time teacher was approved and Mrs Newsum joined the staff. Also in 1970 Miss McKearney retired and Miss V. Goodhind was selected from a shortlist otherwise consisting of all male candidates. Mr R. Robinson was appointed in 1971 as junior teacher and as Deputy Head in 1980. This was because the managers were convinced that with the increased size of the school it needed the influence of a male teacher. In April 1974 Miss Daisy Tidmarsh retired after forty-three years' service. Typically she asked for no formal presentation party but she received gifts from managers, colleagues, present and past pupils and the Parish Council in recognition of her unique contribution to the village.

Changes in the school continued. The building of an extra classroom and multi-purpose hall onto the new school nucleus was completed on 5 November 1984 and the old school was converted into two houses and a small craft shop. Miss Vera Goodhind retired in August 1988 after eighteen years' devoted service, when Mrs V. Church succeeded her as headmistress.

RELIGION

Since 1933 St Martin de Tours at Woolstone has been Gotherington's parish church. The rector lived in Woolstone until September 1971, when the rectory was moved to a new house in Malleson Road. Church services took place in the church room at Ivyville, Malleson Road until 1968 when they moved to the village hall where family services and a Sunday school are still held. There have been six rectors since 1960. In 1966 the Mothers' Union was formed.

Unlike the parish church, Gotherington Free church has had but three ministers since

1960. Marion Holmes' name has been closely associated with the chapel for the whole of this time. In 1983 there were special services to commemorate its one hundred and fiftieth anniversary. The congregations were very different from those first congregations of craftsmen and labourers who wanted to worship in their own village, but interestingly the chapel is still part of the Countess of Huntingdon's Connexion.

SOCIAL ACTIVITIES

The early part of this chapter described how the village has changed its appearance since 1960. The enlarging of the former Reading Room, the acquisition of a parish playing field and the building of the Boys' Club were all visible signs of increasing social activity in the 1960s and 1970s. This, in turn, mirrored not only the increasing population in the village, but also the arrival of professional people who had more leisure time to spare than the traditional occupations based on agriculture. A whole book could be written on the reasons why so many different organizations and societies were established at this time, but in this section it will be sufficient to record the establishment of some of the large variety of different interest groups, most of which are still flourishing today.

Gotherington Boys' Club came into being in 1960 and was affiliated to the National Association of Boys' Clubs in 1962. It met first in the village hall, then built and moved into its own new building on the playing field in April 1966. Girls were later admitted to Senior Club evenings. Activities included football, physical training, table-tennis, judo, climbing, canoeing, sailing, and angling, plus indoor games and lectures. The club visited adventure centres at Kerne Bridge and Drake's Island. The success of this club is due to the

One of the most active of the present village organizations is the Women's Institute, seen here celebrating its silver jubilee in 1978

hard work and dedication of Rex Rhodes, founder and leader for twenty-five years.

Gotherington Guide Company was formed in 1963 and the 1st Gotherington Brownies in 1966. They were in the Bishop's Cleeve District of the Cheltenham Division and transferred to the Tewkesbury Division in March 1968. Gotherington Cub Scouts were formed in 1968 but disbanded twenty years later when numbers diminished.

Gotherington Evergreen Club was formed in 1964 with an initial grant from the Gloucestershire Old People's Welfare. It continues to meet every Tuesday in the village hall. Membership is open to the over fifties.

Gotherington and District Horticultural Society was formed in 1962. It meets on the third Wednesday in the month except June and August. It organizes shows and outings to horticultural places of interest. In the late 1980s it changed its name to Gotherington Garden Club.

One of the most active organizations in the village is the Recreational Club which was formed in 1961 devoted to the purpose of promoting social events for raising funds for village causes. Regular events include dances, a horse show and gymkhana, auction, summer fayre and fireworks. The proceeds of these events are devoted to the provision of amenities for which public funds are not available. It issues a quarterly news magazine called *Gotherington Topics*.

Gotherington, Woolstone and Oxenton's Women's Institute, although formed back in 1953, continues to thrive, especially its choir under the leadership of Margaret Crompton which has achieved international fame. Gotherington Young Wives' Group formed in 1966 was renamed Gotherington Wives' Group in 1972 and meets on the first Wednesday in each month.

The Triton Players were formed in 1967 to encourage interest in drama through play reading, theatre visits, etc. and putting on stage shows in the village hall. It no longer exists.

A clear symbol of change; barns at Baldwin's Farm which have lost their original functions are now desirable residences. This is another change which occurred during the writing of the book

The Cricket Club was re-formed in 1967 after a break of approximately fifteen years. The Tennis Club was started when the tennis courts on the playing field came into use in 1965, and plays throughout the year. The second court was built in 1971.

TRANSPORT

By 1960 trains no longer stopped at Gotherington station but bus companies have served Gotherington well over the years. A.H. Kearsey's No. 14 service provided sixteen buses in each direction to Cheltenham on weekdays and four on Sundays in the 1950s and 1960s. In later years the company of A.H. Kearsey was bought out by Roy Marchant Coaches, some schedules terminating in the village at the Shutter Inn, others continuing to Gretton, Alderton or Stanway.

In the 1960s/'70s there were four Bristol Omnibus services along the Evesham Road. Between them these services accounted for about thirty buses per day in each direction on weekdays and about fourteen on Sundays. In recent years these services were drastically reduced; the Stratford Blue service was taken over by Springs of Evesham who still run a regular Evesham–Cheltenham service. However, for most people in Gotherington today the main form of transport is the private car.

During the last forty years Gotherington, like many of the surrounding villages has developed into a pleasant residential area for families who rely on breadwinners travelling to Cheltenham, Gloucester and even further afield to Birmingham and London to work. Its transformation from a working village has almost been complete. It has taken on the visual appearance and social activities of a professional community and one has to look hard to find remnants of a rural past and a vanishing, if not quite vanished, rural way of life. This chapter has sought to describe these changes and bring the history of the village to its close in our own day.

References

This chapter has been written from personal observation and from information given by present inhabitants of the village.

Index of Places in Gotherington